The First Great
Train Robbery

The First Great
Train Robbery

David C. Hanrahan

ROBERT HALE · LONDON

ISBN 978-0-7090-9040-3

Robert Hale Limited
Clerkenwell House
Clerkenwell Green
London EC1R 0HT

www.halebooks.com

A catalogue record for this book is available from the British Library

2 4 6 8 10 9 7 5 3 1

Typeset by e-type, Liverpool
Printed and bound in the UK by the MPG Books Group,
Bodmin and King's Lynn

Contents

Acknowledgements

This book would not have been possible without the help of a great number of people and institutions. My thanks go to the following: the James Hardiman Library, National University of Ireland, Galway, and in particular Special Collections and Inter-Library Loans; Mary Evans Picture Library, especially Mark Vivan; the National Archives, Kew; the British Library; the Bodleian Library, Oxford; and the National Portrait Gallery, London. For replying to my queries I would like to thank: the City of London Police; British Transport Police and the British Transport Police History Group, especially Kevin Gordon and Bill Rogerson, MBE; and the National Railway Museum, York. I also want to thank my friends and colleagues at the School of Education, National University of Ireland, Galway, in particular Dr Tony Hall for our many positive and inspiring chats and Professor Keith Sullivan for his ongoing support; all at Robert Hale, especially Alexander Stilwell and Nikki Edwards; and my agent, Robert Dudley, who, as ever, was enthusiastic about this project from the beginning. As always, a special word of thanks and love goes to all my family: Margaret, Aisling, Michael, my mother Mary and my brothers and their families.

CHAPTER 1

London to Dover

————•◦•————

The South Eastern Railway Company, like its competitors, offered the most modern form of transportation that was available to travellers in nineteenth-century Britain. The company's rail line from London first reached Folkestone in the year 1843 and Dover the following year.[1] This new line provided, through Folkestone, the quickest available route to continental Europe. It initiated an efficient and convenient service for passengers: 'an express train leaves the London Bridge Terminus every morning specially for the Folkestone tidal-steamer, conveying the passengers direct to the harbour, where a powerful vessel is waiting to receive them, and in two hours afterwards it lands them on the quay at Boulogne, without any of the inconveniences of embarking or disembarking in small boats.'[2] The South Eastern Railway Company was now able to promise passengers that, having boarded a train in London, they would arrive in Berlin in forty-one hours, Marseilles in forty-six hours or Trieste in one hundred and three hours. The main line from London to Dover represented, like many others, an engineering miracle, with seven tunnels along with 'numerous embankments, deep cuttings, viaducts, and bridges …'[3] One of the advantages of having this fast transport link available from London to the major capitals of Europe was that valuables could now be transported more securely. Frequent shipments of gold and other valuables were transported from London to Paris on this route every week. These shipments passed off uneventfully until the evening of 15 May 1855, when everything changed.

On that particular evening three consignments containing gold, coin and paper currency were due to arrive at London Bridge station on the first leg of their journey to Paris. They were to be transported by the South Eastern Railway on board the mail train to Folkestone, from where they would be shipped across the Channel to Boulogne in France by steamboat, and finally on to Paris by rail. As usual, these boxes would be guarded and transported inside specially made portable iron safes, known to the staff as bullion chests, and their contents sealed and carefully weighed before departure.

Henry Gibson Abel, of Messrs Abel & Co., bullion brokers, based at the Royal Exchange buildings in London, was one of those who needed a consignment of gold transported to Paris that evening. His package consisted of six gold bars. The job of delivering Abel's gold bars to the station was undertaken by the company of John Chaplin Co., of the Spread Eagle, Gracechurch Street, the booking-office keepers to the South Eastern Railway. Chaplin sent one of his most reliable and trusted bullion porters to collect the bars: Thomas Sellins, who had been with the firm for seven years.[4] These six bars of gold were valued at upwards of £6,000.[5] Abel saw his gold bars being packed into the usual type of wooden box for transportation, fastened down with iron hoops and the company seal applied. The initials of his consignee in Paris, 'P.D.', and the numbers '184' were marked clearly on the outside of the box. Sellins then brought the gold back to Chaplin's office and delivered it into his employer's charge. From then on, until Abel's gold was delivered to the station, Chaplin would never be more than two or three yards away from it.[6]

Meanwhile, an employee of Adam Spielman & Co., 79 Lombard Street, delivered another valuable package to Chaplin's that day. It was a consignment of gold coin and it too had to be transported to Paris. Chaplin accepted the consignment and filled out the waybill himself. It was addressed to V.

Spielman of 26 Rue Rivoli in Paris.[7] Spielman's coin was valued at between £700 and £800.[8] One more package was received by Chaplin's. It was a consignment of Californian gold, the property of Messrs Bult & Co., a firm of money-changers based in Cheapside, also bound for Paris.

Chaplin watched as the three valuable boxes were loaded onto a cab for transportation to London Bridge station. He felt confident that no one could have known in advance that the valuables were due for transportation on that particular evening.[9] He accompanied the cab himself, arriving at the station at approximately 7.30 p.m. It was important that a close watch be kept on the valuables at all times, as London Bridge station was a very busy place. Even before you entered the station itself your senses were assaulted by myriad sights, sounds and smells. A station by its very nature draws businesses of various descriptions to it and London Bridge was no exception. To the north, and the area around Tooley Street, there were '… wharfingers, merchants, rope-makers, ship-chandlers, outfitters, engineers', while to the south an abundance of 'tan-yards, fellmongers' warehouses, leather-dressers' shops … wool-warehouses, glue factories' and 'rope-walks'.[10] Once inside the station the frenzy did not end. The South Eastern was only one of a number of railway companies using London Bridge station and they all had booking-offices, luggage-handling systems, locomotives that spewed out copious amounts of steam, and a bustling array of anxious and hurried passengers. This was also the kind of environment that attracted thieves of all kinds, from pickpockets to confidence tricksters.

Once on the platform at the station the boxes containing the gold were handed over formally into the possession of the South Eastern Railway, and the ultimate responsibility of Mr Weatherhead, the stationmaster.[11] Edgar Cox, a clerk in Weatherhead's office, accepted the boxes officially on behalf of the railway company.[12] He knew that boxes delivered in that way by Chaplin's always contained valuable contents and required careful monitoring.[13] They would be transported to

Folkestone on board the 8.30 p.m. London to Dover train that evening.

While still on the platform, the boxes were weighed under Cox's direction, by a colleague called Scanlan. Cox noted down the weights carefully in a book normally kept for the purpose in the stationmaster's office: Abel's box, marked 'P.D. 184', came to 1 cwt 1 qr 16 lb; Spielman's box, 18 lb; and the biggest, Bult's Californian gold, 2 cwt 2 qr 15 lb. Chaplin remained on the platform watching the weighing procedure being carried out by the railway staff. Then John Bailey, a porter with the railway company, arrived with a barrow and brought the three boxes to Weatherhead's office. Once the boxes were placed inside the office, they were officially signed for before being put inside the two specially made portable safes. The largest of the wooden boxes, Bult's, was placed in one of the safes on its own and the two smaller ones were placed together in the other safe. Mr Weatherhead then locked both safes in Bailey's presence.[14] The locks on these safes were state of the art and had been specially made for the South Eastern Railway by the firm of Chubb & Sons, the famous lock-makers based at St Paul's Churchyard, London. Each safe had two locks. The same two keys would open both safes, and duplicate sets of keys were kept at London Bridge station, in Folkestone and on the steamboat. Cox kept the wooden boxes in his sight all of the time between their arrival at the station and their being locked inside the safes.[15]

As the time of departure approached, the safes were carried outside Weatherhead's office and '8.30', denoting the time of departure, was written on them in large figures. At five or ten minutes past eight, Bailey brought them from outside Weatherhead's office directly to the train. James Burgess, the railway guard on duty that night, helped Bailey to load them onto his van, the so-called brake van, located towards the front of the train. The valuable cargo would now be under Burgess's supervision throughout the journey to Folkestone. It took Bailey two trips to get both safes to the train.[16]

John Kennedy was working as the underguard to James

Burgess on the 8.30 p.m. train that night. Kennedy had been a loyal and trusted employee of the South Eastern Railway Company for thirteen years. That night he took up his position on the platform three-quarters of an hour before the train was due to depart. While Burgess took charge of his van and the gold, Kennedy supervised the loading of the hinder van, located towards the rear of the train. As head guard, it was Burgess's responsibility to take any parcels or packages from the porters and supervise their loading onto the train. According to Kennedy there were 'a good many passengers that night' so he was very busy.[17] Before the train left the station, Burgess told him to look around the train to ensure that all the doors were locked and the carriages coupled. This task kept Kennedy occupied for around a quarter of an hour. Everything was ready for departure on time; the passengers were on board and the luggage and other cargo had all been loaded, including the two portable iron safes with their valuable contents. The 8.30 p.m. train to Dover pulled out of London Bridge station.

CHAPTER 2

The Same as Any Other Night

————•◦•————

As the train made its way to Dover via Folkestone, Kennedy, the underguard, got out at every station along the way to load and unload luggage. It was the duty of the senior guard, Burgess, to deliver any parcels on board to the relevant stations. He would get out and give them either to the station-master or a porter. If there was no such person present on the platform he would have to take them into the station office himself. Before the train pulled away from any station along the line the correct procedure was for Kennedy, whose van was at the back of the train, to signal that he was ready to leave by holding up a light. Then Burgess should signal in reply and the train would be permitted to move off from the station. In practice, however, these were two experienced guards and they seldom stood on ceremony. Burgess would frequently allow the train to start without receiving any signal from his colleague. Later, Kennedy could not remember if he had received a signal back from Burgess at every station on that particular night, but he thought he probably did at one or two. Kennedy was busy enough with his own work and did not notice how many stations Burgess had got out at, or even if there were many parcels to be delivered on that particular night. In fact, the two men never even glimpsed each other once during the journey. They only saw each other again when they reached the end of the line at Dover station. As far as Kennedy was aware everything had passed off smoothly during the trip, including the unloading of the bullion safes at Folkestone. It seemed a routine journey, like many others that these two guards had taken before. 'I took no notice whether there was anything particular about that journey,' Kennedy would later say, '... it was the same as any other night.'[1]

Kennedy was right; nothing did seem unusual. At Folkestone the normal procedures were carried out. When the train arrived at the upper station the two bullion safes were removed by a porter called Richard Hart and a night-watchman named Cook, under the supervision of Burgess. As the train pulled away on its final short leg of the journey to Dover, the safes were loaded onto a truck and taken away by Hart and Cook for delivery to John Spicer, the night-watchman at the harbour. Hart and Cook did not notice anything unusual that night and they never left the safes unattended on their way from the train to the harbour booking-office.

When they reached the booking-office, Spicer took over responsibility for the safes throughout the night. He made sure that they were not moved and that nobody had access to them. Right across from the booking-office was the telegraph office. On duty there all that night was a clerk, Robert Mackay, who had actually been in the booking-office when one of the safes was brought in. From his own office Mackay could even see the safes standing there in the booking-office, one on top of the other. He did not notice anything unusual. He saw the safes for the last time when his replacement came on duty at 6 a.m. the following morning. Although he did not actually leave the tele-graph office until 8 a.m., Mackay did not see the safes being removed from the booking-office and taken to the boat.

When John McNie, a police officer with the South Eastern Railway, arrived on duty on the morning of 16 May, Spicer alerted him to the presence of the two safes in the booking-office. They were still there, not tampered with in any way, when Spicer went off duty at half past eight. McNie watched as they were taken from the booking-office and delivered safely on board the *Lord Warden* steamboat bound for Boulogne.

In charge of the *Lord Warden* that day was Captain Paul: the mate was James Golder. There were ninety-nine passengers on board. It was Golder's responsibility to supervise the loading of the bullion safes and he had them placed 'midships, on deck' where they remained, in his clear view, for the entire voyage. He was confident that nobody would be able to interfere with them.[2] He had, as he would later say, his 'eye on them the whole time'.[3] The boat left Folkestone Harbour with its valuable cargo on board at 10.30 a.m. and arrived in Boulogne just after midday. Once again it seemed like a very normal journey with no incidents to report.

The captain of the *Lord Warden* had keys to the safes and, in line with normal security procedures, once the boat had docked French customs officials and railway staff came on board and the safes were opened. The wooden boxes were then removed from the safes for the first time since leaving London. Golder watched as the larger of the wooden boxes, which contained Bult's Californian gold, was taken out of its safe. He was amazed at the 'very bad condition' of the box. The side was so bulged out that he could have pushed his finger inside.[4] Jacques Thoron, one of the French customs employees who boarded the *Lord Warden* that morning, removed one of the smaller boxes from the safe himself. Thoron, like Golder, noticed that one of the boxes was open about the width of his finger and he could see a black and white speckled bag moving about inside. He even gave the box two knocks with his heel in an effort to close it. The boxes were placed on a cart and a plank was laid from the deck of the boat to the quayside, along which the boxes were removed with the rest of the luggage. They were brought directly to the custom-house for inspection and weighing.

Thoron stayed with the boxes until James Hamel Major, an agent at Boulogne to the French railway, arrived at the custom-house. As usual there was no requirement by customs to open the boxes, as they were already being charged at the highest rate of duty. Mr Major also noticed the bad condition of the larger box. It was so bad, in fact, that he had custom-house labourers nail it back into shape. The large box and the small box were then put on a truck for transportation to his office, while the third box was placed outside with the other bales and packages and dragged to his office. He said that on that particular day he watched the boxes all the way to his office, which he did not generally do.[5]

When the French officials weighed the boxes there was something else that ought to have caused them concern; one of the boxes was lighter than it should have been according to the accompanying documentation. But neither this, nor the obvious damage to one of the boxes, seemed to raise any significant suspicions among the French officials. Major was content with the fact that for all of the time that the boxes were in his office they were close by him; he kept the two larger ones right in front of him and the smallest one behind. At about half past six, or a quarter to seven, the boxes were put back on the same truck and taken down to the railway for shipment to Paris. Major did not go with them to the train, but it was normal practice for some members of his staff to do so. The shipment was loaded onto the train at Boulogne for the journey to Paris. On arrival in Paris the three boxes were delivered to their intended destinations, still unopened since they had left London, or so it seemed.

It was the following day, 17 May, when Charlemagne Everard, an assistant at Packham Neuffer & Co., Paris, received his wooden box from Abel & Co. in London. He expected that box to contain six gold bars but, to his horror, when he opened it he found nothing but lead shot and some wood shavings inside.[6] Only now was it realized that a shocking crime had been perpetrated. The following day Major was summoned to Paris to see the evidence on behalf of the French railway company. He saw for himself that the box contained no gold, only small, blue, cotton, chequered bags containing nothing more valuable than lead shot and 'a few wood shavings'.[7] 'One bag in the middle had been cut through with a knife; the box being apparently too full for the lid to lie down and the shot had spread, and was mixed with the bags'.[8]

Reports soon came in that the other two boxes delivered that night were also missing their valuables. When Abel's box and its contents were weighed, Major noted that it was almost exactly the same weight as he had recorded at Boulogne, which, as far as the French were concerned, proved that it had not been tampered with anywhere between Boulogne and Paris. What is more, Major examined the lead shot and declared it to be of English origin. He discovered this, he claimed, by biting it. He said that English shot was 'much softer' than French.[9] This, of course, also placed the blame for the loss of the gold very firmly on the English side. On the other hand, there were other reports stating that pages from a French pamphlet had been found inside one of the boxes.[10] Accusations of blame began to be hurled from one country to the other.

When the authorities began to consider the size of the haul that had gone missing, it came to a considerable amount. Apart from one hundred bars of gold, it included: '… 10 orders for the payment of 1,000*l.*; 10 warrants for the payment of 1,000*l.*, and money to the amount of 1,000*l*'.[11] It came to a total value calculated to be somewhere between twelve and fourteen thousand pounds. No one knew how or by whom the valuables had been stolen.

CHAPTER 3

Feloniously Abstracted

A t first the authorities could not countenance the idea that the valuables had been stolen from a moving train, protected by two iron safes fitted with modern Chubb locks. Surely modern technology would allow no such occurrence? They were not the first, nor the last, to assume that the latest technology would offer protection against crime. The board of the South Eastern Railway Company was summoned at once by its secretary, Samuel Smiles, and it was decided to offer a reward of £300 for information leading to the capture of the thieves and the recovery of the gold. Disagreement raged on between the British and French sides concerning whose jurisdiction in which the gold had actually been stolen. Smiles was one of those who pushed the idea that it 'had been committed by foreigners on the French railway'.[1] This was a view shared by many on the British side: 'It is supposed that so well planned a scheme could not have been executed in the rapid passage by railway from London to Folkestone.'[2]

The first time that the general public found out about this major crime was when a short notice appeared in *The Times* of 21 May 1855. By now the idea being pursued was that the robbery could have taken place at Folkestone before the valuables were loaded onto the boat: 'A serious robbery is stated to have been committed in the transmission of specie to Paris, boxes having been opened and lead substituted for gold. It is believed to have happened at Folkestone, and the amount taken is said to be

12.000*l.* or 14,000*l.*'³ A more extensive article, including the announcement of a reward being offered by the railway, appeared the following day:

THREE HUNDRED POUNDS REWARD.

Whereas a large quantity of GOLD, in bars and in American coin, was FELONIOUSLY ABSTRACTED from THREE BOXES, dispatched from London to Paris on Tuesday, the 15th inst., via the South Eastern Railway, Folkstone, Boulogne, and the Northern Railway of France; This is to give notice that a reward of £300 will be paid to any person who shall give such information as shall lead to the apprehension of the offender or offenders and recovery of the property or a proportionate sum for any part so recovered.

The Times, 22 May, 1855

The question was, had anything unusual or suspicious happened that night? Henry Williams, a booking clerk at Dover station, was working on the night of 15 May 1855 when the 8.30 p.m. mail train from London arrived at around eleven o'clock. On the face of it, there did not seem to be anything out of the ordinary about that night. The up-train to London was due to leave Dover at 2 a.m. as usual. It was an express train with only First Class carriages and that night, as normally happened, it would only carry a few passengers. Williams issued only two tickets for the train and both were bought by an elderly gentleman. One was for himself and the other for a young man who Williams thought could be aged anywhere from twelve to twenty years. They looked like father and son. Burgess and Kennedy were both in the office at the time, and all the railway employees present were having a chat. The only other slightly notable event that had occurred on that night was that, as Williams was issuing the tickets to the old man, two other men had walked through the office and towards the train without buying tickets from him. These men carried bags in their hands and one of them 'was of light complexion' and the other 'dark'.

These men were met at the door of the booking-office by Joseph Witherden, a porter. He asked them if he could carry their bags to the train but they declined. By the way they carried them, the bags seemed quite heavy to Witherden. One of the men was taller than the other and they both wore cloaks and slouched hats, although Witherden could not remember if the cloaks were long or short. Witherden asked them about their tickets for the train and they showed him two blue 'first class tickets by way of Ostend'.[4] He asked them if their bags had passed through customs and they told him that they had come through the previous evening. He was slightly puzzled by their story, as he thought that the Ostend boat had not come in early enough that night to catch the 2 a.m. train. He opened the carriage door for them and one of them handed him some money. They entered the carriage and the one who had given him the money sat nearest to the door. Witherden's interaction with the men lasted only about two or three minutes. After that, they were kept waiting on board the train for a quarter of an hour or twenty minutes before it pulled out of the station.[5]

Robert Clark, who was a waiter at the Dover Castle Hotel, a position he took up in April 1855, also remembered two men he had never seen before coming to the hotel soon after he first moved there. It could very well have been the night in question. They arrived one night around eleven o'clock. As far as he could recollect, they had two bags with them. He remembered them in particular because when they were leaving they asked him to put some brandy in a soda water bottle for them to take away. Around 1.30 a.m., they left to catch the 2 a.m. train to London.

Matthew Dickenson was a porter with the South Eastern Railway at London Bridge station. On the morning of 16 May 1855 the 2 a.m. train from Dover was due in at 4.30 a.m.[6] There were not more than four passengers on board that night. Dickenson opened one of the carriages and let two men out. One was a little taller than the other and one had a darker complexion. Dickenson knew that the one who stepped out first was carrying a bag but he could not remember if the other one was. They had no other luggage. As far as he could remember, there was no luggage on the train that particular morning. Dickenson spoke to one of these men, who had a large cape on, dark hair and whiskers. He asked the man if he wanted a cab, but the man declined. Something about the interaction must have struck him as odd though, because he remarked on it to his colleague, a porter called William Woodhouse: 'They won't allow me to get them a cab,' he said, 'they say they will get one for themselves.'[7] The last sight that Dickenson caught of these two men was of them walking down the platform together.

Woodhouse's duty was to unload the luggage from the train. As far as he could remember, none of the passengers had any luggage that morning, apart from what they were carrying. He remembered seeing three passengers exit the train: two of them walked up the platform together and the other followed a minute or two later. Of the two walking together, one was rather taller than the other, but Woodhouse was about twelve or fourteen yards away from them and would not be able to recognize them again.

It was perhaps a seventy or eighty yard walk from the train, along the platform and out of the station. As usual, two policemen were on duty at the exit that night.[8] As a courtesy to passengers, one of the policemen would hail horse-drawn cabs for people, if required, and the other would call out the destination to which the passenger wanted to be taken.[9] But that night, neither policeman could remember anything remarkable about any of the passengers.

Had these two unidentified men who travelled from Dover to London that night anything to do with the robbery? No one knew. For now, the whole thing remained a mystery.

CHAPTER 4

The Investigation

The crime had come as a shock to the authorities and it threw them, as Samuel Smiles, the Secretary of the South Eastern Railway, put it, 'into consternation'.[1] At that time, although there were always pickpockets and suchlike trying to ply their trade on the trains, a crime of this nature was unprecedented. There had been a robbery of a much smaller type attempted on the Great Western Railway on 2 January 1849. This incident concerned two men, Henry Pool and Edward Nightingale, who attempted to rob a train that was transporting mail from London. Pool had at one time been a guard on the Great Western Railway and so knew the procedures. The two men boarded the train at Bristol and soon made their way to the mail tender, which was temporarily unguarded. Included in the items that they stole from the mailbags were twelve letters, six rings to the value of £140 and a £2 watch case. Unfortunately for the two culprits the crime was discovered when the train stopped at Bridgwater and the guard noticed that the mailbags had been tampered with. This meant that the suspects were very quickly identified, even though Pool had done his best to hide himself by wearing a false moustache and a hat to cover his face. On arrival in Exeter, both they and the carriage in which they had been travelling were searched. The authorities found a number of incriminating items including two masks, 'a pair of false mustachios' and, under the seat on which Pool had been sitting, the stolen letters.[2] It transpired that the earlier up-train to

London that day had also been robbed in a similar manner. The men tried to claim that they were not travelling together and did not even know each other, but witnesses soon came forward to say that they had seen the two men together on the days leading up to the crime. Both were tried for the crime in Exeter in March 1849, and sentenced to fifteen years transportation. Their small crime was not, however, accorded the same rank in criminal history as the train robbery of 1855.

The South Eastern Railway's own police force had begun their investigation into the robbery of the gold and other valuables immediately. Also involved in trying to work out this criminal puzzle were the Metropolitan Police force, in particular Inspectors Williamson and Thornton, and a number of other English police forces, along with the French authorities. It was hoped that the widely advertised reward of £300 would lead to information and quick arrests. Hundreds of people were questioned, including the railway, harbour and boat employees who were on duty that night.

The idea that the robbery must have taken place on French soil persevered for some time and on that basis the railway company refused to pay the compensation claims of those who had lost out financially. One of these claimants, Abel, decided to bring an action against the South Eastern Railway because they continued to resist his claim for compensation on the grounds that his box of gold was stolen between Boulogne and Paris. Their attitude infuriated him: '... they kept us out of our money the whole of that time,' he said, 'which we did not think very gentlemanly....'3

Since such a crime had never been committed before, most people still found it very difficult to accept that a modern train in transit had been robbed, so they continued to look for other possible explanations; for example, concern was raised about the fact that the valuable cargo had been left overnight in the booking-office in Folkestone, rather than in a more appropriate strongroom. Many still wondered if this was where the robbers had gained access to it. In the end, seeing as one of the boxes was lighter than it should have been on its arrival in France, and one of them had been quite clearly damaged, people were forced to accept the truth that the gold was already missing by the time the safes reached France. They also had to accept the rather unpalatable fact that the most modern form of transport available, the train, had fallen victim to one of the oldest of human activities, theft. This acceptance of reality was signified by the fact that in December 1855 the compensation payment for Abel was agreed. The only outstanding questions now were how, and by whom, the gold and other valuable items had been stolen from a train in transit?

It emerged that the representatives of the Chubb lock company were extremely unhappy about something that they had discovered. They had been asked to examine the bullion safes in the wake of the robbery to look for signs of a forced entry. Their locks were, it seems, fitted with 'detector contrivances' that should have given an indication had they been interfered with. No such indication was found.[4] They did, however, find something else that shocked them more. They discovered that it had become standard practice for the South Eastern Railway employees to use only one of the locks on each of the bullion safes. In order to make access quicker and easier, the staff were only using one key and one lock. In fact, on investigation, the experts from Chubb found that the second locks on every one of the safes had become rusted and ineffective through lack of use. This was completely in contravention of Chubb's recommended practice.

Then, suddenly, it emerged that a credible suspect had been discovered. Public attention became focused on the story of a man called Samuel Seal. Seal, of '1, Little Street, Andrew Street, Seven Dials' was described as a well-dressed, middle-aged, bullion merchant.[5] He was now about to become a prime suspect in a most serious crime. John Davis Sutcliffe was working in his sister's business at Long Acre on Saturday, 19 May 1855, when Seal, whom he had known by sight for eight or nine years, entered the premises. Mr Seal proceeded to tell Sutcliffe that 'he had a quantity of Australian gold, which had come from Melbourne, and ... was very good'.[6] He said that he had about one hundred ounces in all. Sutcliffe was interested and made an appointment with Seal to see the gold on the following Monday morning. Seal arrived as agreed and he had five bars of gold in his possession, which Sutcliffe weighed and found came to one hundred and one ounces. Sutcliffe had never seen Australian gold in bars before as, in his experience, it usually came in nuggets. Nevertheless, Seal assured him that it was 'very good' and said: 'I hope you will give me a good price for it.'[7] A small piece was cut off one of the bars for evaluation and Seal went away with the rest. The next morning Seal returned to find out the result of the evaluation, but it had not yet been completed so he had to call again in the afternoon. On his return, Sutcliffe told him that the gold was, in fact, 'of a first-rate quality' and that he was willing to give him '4*l*. 0*s*. 10*d*. per ounce' for it.[8] The following day, when the banks reopened, Sutcliffe paid Seal £409 17s. 1d; for which he received a receipt.[9]

The next day Seal returned once more saying that he had met a captain down at the docks 'who had a very large quantity of Australian gold', of which he produced a small sample. This time Sutcliffe, on examination of the gold, told him straight away that this 'was not Australian gold'.[10] Seal argued that it was, claiming that it was granulated Australian gold. Sutcliffe asked him to leave it so that he could examine it more closely, but Seal said that he would have to go for instructions before he could agree to do that. He left and never returned.

Seal instead called at the business premises of Samuel Montague, a bullion merchant based at 51 Cornhill.[11] He was dealt with, in the first instance, by the manager, Ellis Abraham Franklin, who soon grew suspicious of his customer. Seal produced two ounces of granulated gold, which he said was a sample from a larger amount. He said he wanted it 'melted and assayed'.[12] As the staff of Montague's examined the gold, Seal proceeded to give references regarding his respectability, even though he had not been asked to do so, which aroused the manager's suspicions even more. One of the places he mentioned at which his character could be vouched for was the diamond merchants Messrs Josephs, Meyers & Co. of Leadenhall Street.[13] Although Seal once again claimed that the gold had come from Australia, in the professional opinion of the proprietor, Montague, in view of its quality and condition this was not the case.[14] Then, when Seal was asked to leave the sample after him, he refused to do so, saying that he would rather take it with him and return later with the full amount. All of this Montague and his staff found very suspicious, especially 'in consequence of hearing of the recent [train] robbery'.[15] They decided to contact the authorities. When Seal's reference with Messrs Josephs, Meyers & Co. was checked out by the police it transpired that they 'had known him some years ago, but had lost sight of him in the way of business, and had had no transactions with him for many years'.[16] When Seal returned with the gold he found himself confronted by a police detective called Michael Haydon:

> I told him I belonged to the police, and perhaps he would be kind enough to give me his name, address, and occupation, which he accordingly did. I told him I assumed him to be an honest man, but a very extensive robbery of gold having taken place, I should like him to give an account of how he came possessed of the gold. He then said he was a diamond merchant and bullion dealer.[17]

When Haydon went to Seal's business premises he found it to be tobacconist and confectioners.[18] Seal told Haydon that a few days earlier a gentleman called Williams had walked into his shop. He had been acquainted with this man for a short period, six years earlier.[19] Williams asked Seal if he would be interested in buying some gold. When Seal agreed, they set off to the London Docks together. When they got there, Williams went away for a short while before returning with the bag of gold. The two men then returned to Seal's shop, where Seal weighed the gold and paid Williams £3 10s an ounce for it, or £360 in total.[20] Haydon asked Seal if he knew where Williams was now and his answer seemed dubious: 'He said no – that Williams, upon receiving the money, said that it was his intention to go to Liverpool immediately to get back to Australia.'[21] Furthermore, Seal told the detective that he 'kept no books' and there was no written account of the transaction. Understandably, Haydon was not satisfied with these answers and so he arrested Seal on suspicion of being 'in possession of 106 ounces of gold, reasonably suspected to have been stolen or unlawfully obtained'.[22] It was widely believed that Seal and his gold were connected with the train robbery. He was brought to a hearing before Alderman Wire and Sir R.W. Carden at the Mansion House, refused bail and remanded in custody. A number of court appearances followed along with three weeks in custody for Seal. However, in the end the case against him fell apart. At the hearing in the Mansion House one witness, Mr T. Rance, an employee of Messrs Abel & Co., said that their gold marked 'P.D. 184', which was stolen in the train robbery, was nothing like that in the possession of Seal: 'That which I packed was nearly pure gold; it was better than standard. Its gross weight was 2,125½ ounces ... This is not like our gold, and is inferior to it ... I cannot at all tell what this is – it is not like our gold....'[23] In the end, the authorities were forced to concede that they could produce no credible evidence linking Seal or his gold with the train robbery and he was discharged by the Lord Mayor.[24]

Once again the authorities appeared to be back where they had started; they had an unsolved crime and no suspects to charge. The embarrassing debacle of the train robbery prompted the board of the South Eastern Railway to make some changes to personnel. According to Smiles: '... it must be admitted that things had been allowed to go ... a great deal too far, and that a clearance of some of the incapables (to say the least of them) must soon be made'.[25] One of those new people employed was a young solicitor called John Charles Rees. He was appointed to the position of company law clerk and one of his responsibilities would be the supervision of the investigation into the robbery.

Although he was, according to Smiles, 'comparatively inexperienced', the secretary had confidence in him.[26] Perhaps this was based on the record of Rees's father, who was a solicitor with a good reputation and had, it seems, 'at one time ... been able to effect a discovery in a similar case'.[27] After his appointment Rees, accompanied by his father, paid a visit to Folkestone. They suspected that the stationmaster there must have been involved in the robbery and the elder Mr Rees, in particular, tried to intimidate the truth out of the man: 'Old Mr Rees fixed his penetrating eye upon the station-master, who, he thought, quailed before his glance, as much as to say, 'Ah! You have found me out, have you?'[28] This too, however, turned out to be a fruitless line of enquiry. No connection between the stationmaster at Folkestone and the robbery was ever established.

Around Good Friday 1856 Rees decided to send for Burgess, the train guard, in order to ask him some questions about what had happened on the night of the robbery.[29] He told Burgess that he should make efforts not to be seen by anyone when he arrived, so as not to arouse suspicions about himself. According to Rees, he failed to get any significant information from Burgess at this meeting: 'The general effect of his answers to my questions was that he had nothing to disclose, that he knew nothing whatever of the matter'.[30] Although Rees said that he wrote down the contents of that interview, he claimed a few months later that he thought the paper was no longer in existence.[31] The authorities decided to keep an eye on Burgess but, during that time, he never engaged in anything more riotous than the singing of songs about Dick Turpin in a Dover public house. [32] He was never seen in the company of anyone suspicious. Whether or not Rees and his colleagues were convinced by Burgess's claims of innocence, they had no evidence against him.

A year passed and it looked to the public as if the investigators had spent an inordinate amount of time, energy and money on the case and yet, it seemed, had failed to come up with anything conclusive. Apart from Seal, they had made no arrests and did not seem to have any credible suspects. It looked as if they had no idea how, or by whom, the valuables had been stolen. In the end it would take the activities of a professional thief in London to bring about, inadvertently, the circumstances that would throw light upon the mystery of the Great Train Robbery of 1855.

CHAPTER 5

Dishonour Among Thieves

————•————

Edward Robert Agar was thirty-eight years of age in 1855.[1] He was small and thin with an oval-shaped face, light brown hair and grey eyes that were described as 'keen' and 'bright'.[2] His criminal past had left its physical marks on him in the form of scars on his left temple and on his upper lip just below his left nostril. He was unethical, unscrupulous and crooked. Although described as 'semi-literate', he was criminally ingenious.[3] One of his skills was as a locksmith, with a particular penchant for making keys with which to open other people's safes. When the iron safe of Messrs Rogers, a bank located in Clement's Lane, was opened using a duplicate key and robbed of £45,000, Agar was widely reputed to have been the culprit responsible.[4]

Such bank robberies were highly risky, however, and Agar's crime of choice was forgery. His other great gift, aside from the opening of safes, was the production of fake cheques using engraved plates, which he then made out for substantial sums of money bearing a signature forged with considerable artistry. His usual practice was to dupe a young subject into aiding and abetting him in the crime. This was intended to keep him one step away from any potential arrest and it proved to be most successful. He would place an advertisement for a clerk, or contact those who had advertised their services for such a situation, and then use them to effect the scam. Ironically, these people would be chosen for their honest appearance and character. This innocent third party would be sent to present one of Agar's forged cheques at a bank and have it cashed. Agar always had an accomplice observing the transaction from a distance, just in case the scam was detected and his 'clerk' was arrested. If that happened, Agar would have plenty of time to destroy any evidence and, if necessary, escape.[5] Providing all went well, and the innocent party was not arrested, they would return the money to Agar as instructed and perhaps receive a small fee. Their hopes of being employed on a long-term basis were always, of course, dashed.

Not as dangerous as bank robbery perhaps, but Agar was well aware that even this crime was not completely risk free. One of his jobs in 1853 had gone terribly wrong.[6] On that occasion Agar sent one of his stooges into the bank of Messrs Barnett & Hoare in Lombard Street to present a forged cheque. Initially all went well and the bank official paid over the amount of £850. But as soon as Agar's man left the premises, the cheque was discovered to be a forgery. The bank officials acted quickly and sent the serial numbers from the notes that they had just given out to the man on to the Bank of England. When one of Agar's accomplices, the thirty-year-old William Nash, went into the Bank of England to exchange those same notes for gold, he was arrested.[7] He was tried at the Old Bailey and sentenced to fifteen years transportation. Luckily for Agar no evidence linking the crime back to him was discovered and he remained at large.

Agar may have escaped punishment in the Nash affair, but this mishap taught him a lesson; after that he began making frequent trips to America in order to distribute some of those notes he thought most likely to be traceable in England.[8] With Nash now out of action, Agar began to work with another accomplice, William Pierce.[9] As long as he could evade arrest, and even if a transaction went wrong every now and then and he lost an accomplice like Nash, this criminal scam was highly lucrative for Agar. By August 1855, however, Agar's personal relationships had become complicated and that was about to get him into a whole lot of trouble.

A woman called Fanny Bolam Kay was, arguably, the love of Agar's life.[10] He was not, however, always loyal to her and their relationship could be a tumultuous one. Fanny had once worked as an assistant at the Tunbridge station refreshment bar but she was dismissed from her job in 1852. No doubt her heavy drinking was a factor in her dismissal but so too, she admitted, was her involvement with a man.[11] After she lost her job she moved back to her mother's place in London for a few months and got a job at Crosse & Blackwell's in Soho Square. When she left her mother's house she went to live at Johnson Street, Somers Town. She was only twenty-one years of age in 1853 when she began the most important relationship of her life, with Agar. She was first introduced to Agar in the Green Man public house in Tooley Street near London Bridge station by the train guard James Burgess. When she walked in there that day, Burgess and Agar were sitting together talking. Fanny had a difficult personality, a serious drinking habit and a record of many romantic encounters with men. Nevertheless, she and Agar hit it off and they were soon having an intimate relationship. Fanny and Agar moved in together on 11 June 1853.[12] Because of Agar's criminal activities they moved around a lot, living first at 'Margaret Street, Oxford Street' and then moving to a succession of places including Southampton, Greenwich, Kent Road, Prospect Place, Brighton and Vauxhall.[13] Fanny gave birth to a baby boy, named Edward Robert after his father, on 7 July, 1854.[14] In December of that year they moved to Cambridge Villas in Shepherd's Bush.

In his own way, Agar loved Fanny and his son very much, but he could never be the conventional, faithful partner and father. His latest trouble came about because, during a period of estrangement from Fanny, he began a relationship with another woman, called Emily Campbell. Within a few months he had moved out of their house in Shepherd's Bush and was living instead with Emily in Paddington. The problem was that Emily had previously been the intimate partner of another shady London character, a man called Bill Humphries, and the jilted lover decided to lay a trap for Agar. Humphries was aware of Agar's activities as a forger and he came up with a plan to have him charged with passing one of his forged cheques.

William Smith, of 36 Blenheim Street, Chelsea, who described himself as 'a carpenter and cabinet maker', was working for Humphries in the summer of 1855. He became central to what happened next. It was while working at Humphries' house around the middle of June that Smith first met Agar. Smith knew him as 'Mr Jenkins'. He would call to the house and he was, according to Smith, 'on friendly terms' with Humphries.[15] Agar noticed the tattoo on Smith's arm and struck up a conversation with him about it. They discussed Smith's travels abroad to exotic places such as 'Calcutta, St. Helena, and the Cape of Good Hope'. Agar told him that he had never been to the East, but had been to America and the West Indies.[16] As Agar used to come to the house three or four times a week and Humphries was often out when he called, he would sit in 'the front office' and spend time chatting with Smith. According to Smith he sometimes stayed there 'the major part of the day'.[17]

Agar may have liked Smith, but it is more likely that he was merely evaluating his potential as a criminal associate or stooge. In any event, Agar soon started asking Smith to do small jobs for him. In June he asked him 'to take a small box for him to Pickfords booking office in Oxford Street ...'.[18] Smith did as he was asked but, strangely, noticed Agar standing and watching him from the other side of the street. The task was, no doubt, a first test of Smith's reliability. One day Agar saw Smith doing a drawing of a door that he was fitting for Humphries and he remarked to him: 'You seem handy with your pen, old fellow; would you like to leave off carpentering?'[19] When Smith said that he would, Agar told him that he might be able to do something for him. According to Smith, Agar soon had another job for him. This time he had to deliver ten sovereigns to a 'stout' and 'very dark' man wearing spectacles in a coffee-house in Orange Street: '... I was to ask him if he was waiting to see Mr A– and if he said yes, I was to ask him what he was waiting to receive; and if he said 10*l*., I was to give him the ten sovereigns.'[20] Smith went there and the 'stout' man was present as Agar had said. It all passed off smoothly; Smith gave the man the money and left immediately. He then met Agar at Tom's Coffee House in Holborn as instructed and Agar paid him a sovereign for his trouble.

Agar's next task for Smith was even simpler. This time it merely involved looking after a package. It was heavy, but only 'about four inches wide, eight or nine inches long, and about half an inch thick'.[21] Agar did not reveal what was inside but the dimensions had a great similarity to the plates he used for forging cheques. It was important enough for Agar to want to know Smith's address in case, he said, he needed it back in a hurry. After about a fortnight the two men met at The Black Horse in Coventry Street, Haymarket, and Agar took the package back. They arranged to meet again the following evening at the same place and Agar gave him another similar package to look after.

On 4 August 1855 Smith moved to 61 Theobalds Road and on that day he met Agar by accident in Southampton Row. Agar said that he had another job coming up for him soon. He asked Smith if he 'had ever transacted business at a bankers'.[22] When Smith told him that he had, Agar said that he wanted him to present a cheque for payment. They met a number of times after that to discuss the job, usually on the street outside Tom's Coffee House. Smith would walk up and down the street until Agar arrived. The job may have seemed simple enough, but Agar gave Smith precise instructions regarding the passing of the cheque: he was to present it to the bank staff in the usual way and if anything went wrong and they started asking him questions, Smith was to say that he got the cheque from a 'Captain Pellatt, of the Euston Hotel'. Agar concocted a detailed story for Smith to tell in such a circumstance. He took great care to ensure that Smith would get everything right, asking him if he understood what he had to do and getting him to repeat the instructions back to him.

When Agar was happy that Smith was ready, he gave him the forged cheque, which was made out for £700 drawn on the account of Mr John Deverell and payable to 'W. Pellatt, Esq. or bearer'.[23] He even provided him with a canvas bag in which to carry the money received. The cheque was dated for the following Wednesday and Agar told him that he was to take it to the bank on that day. Agar said that he would wait for him to return with the money in Southampton Row, Bedford Square or Russell Square. He would be walking around that area.

It seems unlikely but, according to Smith's story, he only at this point began to realize that he might be engaged in criminality of some sort: 'I began to suspect,' he said, '... that Agar was not so honest a man as he ought to be....'[24] Smith claimed that he was so worried about it that he decided to confide in his boss, Humphries. He said that Humphries advised him to go to Richard Mullens, solicitor to the associated bankers of the City of London, and tell him everything about what Agar had asked him to do: '... Humphries told me that Mr Mullens was the attorney to the bankers, and that he was the proper solicitor for anything of that kind – Humphries at once lent himself to the discovery, and did all he could to suggest the means of discovery....'[25]

Smith did admit that by then Humphries and Agar were not so friendly: '... he did not behave as if he were a very intimate friend of Agar's....'[26] This was because Emily had by now deserted him for Agar. She had moved out of Humphries' house and was now living with Agar. When he heard Smith's story, Mullens knew that he was on to something big. Forgery of this kind was a serious problem in the city and he realized that Smith's arrival in his office was an extremely lucky development. He decided, with Smith's help, to set a trap for Agar. He organized what would in later times be called a 'stake-out' or 'sting operation'. Smith was instructed to do just as Agar had asked. On the day in question, Smith arrived at Stevenson & Salt's Banking House in Lombard Street just after three o'clock. Two officers, John Forrester and Henry Goddard, were placed in Glyn's Banking House on the opposite side of the street. Forrester was a policeman and Goddard a retired police officer who had been hired by Mullens to assist.[27] Mullens himself was sitting inside the window of Stevenson & Salt's. About a quarter of an hour earlier, from the window of the bank, Mullens had observed a suspicious man standing on the pavement across the street smoking a cigar. Mullens did not recognize him, but that man was Agar's accomplice, Pierce. Then a cab drew up and a conversation took place, 'very earnestly for a very short time', between the man on the street and the man in the cab.[28] Then the man in the cab got out and walked away. Mullens believed that the man in the cab was Agar.

When Smith entered the bank, Mullens took the cheque and the canvas bag from him. He then filled the bag up with coins and handed it back to him. Neither Smith nor Agar knew it but, just in case anything went wrong, Mullens had filled the bag with farthings and 'marked pieces of paper', instead of sovereigns.[29] Smith then exited the bank. Outside the door, in clear view of the street, he put the bag in his breast pocket as he had been instructed by Mullens. Mullens knew that Agar, or perhaps his associate, would be watching, and he wanted Smith to make it obvious that he had successfully cashed the cheque: '... I gave him some directions as to putting it into his pocket as he went out – he carried the bag in his hand until he got outside the door, and I saw him stand on the pavement, and put it into his breast pocket – any person standing about would have an opportunity of seeing him.'[30] Smith then walked to Southampton Row, arriving there at around four o'clock. He walked around for a while, waiting for Agar. When Agar did not arrive, he went into a public house 'by Boswell Court' and bought himself a glass of ale.[31] Then, unexpectedly, Humphries arrived and went into the same public house. Evidently he had also been following events from somewhere near. Two of Mullens's men, Goddard and a man called Jonathan Thorogood, went in after him and saw him talking to Smith. Goddard heard the interaction between them: '... when Humphries came in he said, "Oh, here you are," and he laid hold of Smith's arm, and said, "Come this way," and took him into the parlour.'[32] Goddard and Thorogood followed them into the parlour, where the conversation continued: 'He will not be here now he will be at my office at 5 o'clock,' Humphries said. 'Have you got it?' he asked, referring to the bag of money. Smith told him that he had, gesturing to the relevant pocket. 'Pull it out,' Humphries said, 'and let us see it.'[33] At that suggestion Thorogood thought that he had better intervene in this foolish conversation: 'No, not in my presence,' he said, 'for if you take it I shall take you into custody; my instructions are to take the first man that Smith gives the bag to.'[34] This brought the conversation to a close and Humphries left abruptly. The whole interaction had lasted for about six or seven minutes.[35] Shortly afterwards Smith went back out onto the street.

Humphries had been wrong about Agar not coming. Agar may have been observing his man from a distance all the time, and finally, when he felt confident that it was safe to approach, he walked up to Smith between the corner of Bedford Row and Theobalds Road. The two men shook hands. Agar asked Smith whether everything had gone all right and Smith replied that it had. They walked as they chatted: up Bedford Row into a street that led to Red Lion Square, across the square and down Leigh Street on to Eagle Street and then Kingsgate Street. As they walked, Agar kept looking around and behind him. Then he spotted Goddard and Thorogood and asked: 'Who are those fellows over there?'[36] When Smith said that he did not know, Agar said: 'They are following us, walk this way towards Holborn.'[37] They arrived at Kingsgate Street, Holborn, and, according to Smith, Agar then said: 'Sling me the stuff, and then I will run for it.' He also said: 'How b—y careless you were in putting the bag in your pocket at the bank in Lombard Street.'[38] Smith then handed him the bag and Agar ran. According to Smith he was shouting instructions at him as he did so: '… he told me to go into a baker's shop, and he would run to the fields, meaning Lincoln's Inn Fields – he pointed to a baker's shop at the corner, so that I should not run the same way as he did….'[39]

Thorogood chased after Agar 'across Holborn, down New Turnstile into Gate Street, Great Queen Street, Little Queen Street, into Parker Street'.[40] He called 'Stop thief!' after him and a number of people did try to stop him, but without success. Then, suddenly, Agar, sly as ever, adopted a new strategy: when Thorogood entered Parker Street he met him walking towards him boldly, without his hat. When Thorogood grabbed him he said: 'You have made a mistake; Down that way, down that way! ... I have done nothing....'[41] But it was no good, Thorogood recognized him and was not letting him go. Thorogood pointed to Smith and said: 'The fact is, this young man ... has been watched from the banking house, in Lombard Street, and you have received something from him; what have you done with it?'[42]

Agar handed over the bag of money without a struggle. Forrester had by this time arrived on the scene and he took Agar into custody in a shop on Little Queen Street. He told Agar that he was being arrested for forgery. Goddard gave Forrester the bag of money. Presumably to make it look good, the police arrested Smith as well and handcuffed the two of them together. They were still handcuffed together when they were brought to the Mansion House. According to Smith, Agar still had more to say: 'It was your fault that I was taken, through running the same way as I did; but if you stick to me, if it costs me a thousand pounds I will get you out of it.'[43]

Agar was searched and in his possession the police found a key, which was later found to belong to 7 Stanley Place, Paddington.[44] As he attempted to explain himself, Agar's version of events sounded very different to Smith's. He told the police that the whole thing was a frame-up. He said that he had nothing to do with any cheque being presented at the bank. He said that he had an appointment with Humphries at five o'clock that day, in order to receive £235 from him that he had lent to him on the previous Monday. He said that this was why he was standing at the corner of Bedford Row, from where he could see Humphries' house. Then this gentleman called Smith approached him, saying: 'Oh! I am watching for you.' According to Agar, Smith claimed that Humphries had sent him with his money. As they walked along together, Smith handed him the bag of money, which he thought was his £235. By this time they were near Red Lion Square and, Agar had not realized it until then, but they were being followed by two men. When he saw them, Agar said that he asked Smith who they were and Smith told him that he did not know. Then, he said, Smith suddenly told him to run away saying: 'I will stand here, and the officers won't know you are gone.'[45] According to Agar, he was confused and unsure what to do, so he began to run. But as soon as he did, Smith shouted: 'Stop thief!'

Goddard said that once he had Agar in custody he asked him if he had taken a bag from this man and he admitted that he had. He then was asked where it was and Agar gave it to him willingly. When asked how much it contained, Agar said '£200, I believe'. Agar asked Smith about the contents of the bag, in the presence of the police, but Smith just shook his head and said that he did not know. Throughout it all, Agar continued to insist that the whole thing was a frame-up: 'I was completely trepanned into the affair,' he said.[46] He told the police that Humphries was behind it all and he even explained what the man's motive was: '… it was a vindictive feeling,' he told them, 'that was the cause of my being arrested….'[47] The reason was jealousy: 'I was at that time living with a young woman who had lived with Humphreys [sic], and this was the cause of his giving information against me.'[48]

Agar's claims of innocence became even more incredible when Smith handed in to the police the package that Agar had given him for safe keeping. It turned out to contain forged engraving plates for printing cheques from five different banks.[49] That was not all. Also found among his possessions were: '… thirteen pieces of paper, counterfoils of printed cheques, four blank cheques of Hill and Sons, and two of Lacey and Sons Bankers, in Smithfield, forty-nine of the Eastern Bank, Norwich, sixty-nine of Coutts', three sheets of tracing paper, a forged 5*l.* Bank of England note, and a forged 10*l.* Bank of England note, three bank cheques….'[50]

Little wonder that the authorities did not believe Agar's explanation for what had occurred and consequently sent him forward to be tried for the crime of forgery. Nobody knew it yet, but this development would eventually have momentous repercussions for the investigation into the train robbery.

CHAPTER 6

A Fearful Representation

---·•·---

Agar's trial for forgery took place at the Old Bailey on 22 October 1855. Mr Sergeant Ballantine, the counsel for Agar's defence, did his best to discredit Smith as a witness. Admittedly, with his past record there was a lot to attack. Ballantine intimated that a premises at which Smith was once the proprietor, at King's Place in Pall Mall, had been a brothel. Smith claimed it was, strictly speaking, a lodging house and not a brothel, but his claims for the venue's respectability were unconvincing:

> ... I believed there is a distinction between the two – if parties came there to hire a room, to stop for any period, I never asked them their business – the question was never put whether they wanted to stop a night or a week – if any persons wanted to occupy a room, they could do so by paying for it – there were no women kept in the house, - that is, no women for the purpose you imagine – I believe men and women could come and hire a room there for the purposes of fornication whenever they pleased....[1]

It did not help that, later in his evidence, Smith inadvertently used the word 'brothel' himself to describe the establishment.[2] As a means of defence he claimed that he had made very little of his income from that house anyway. Most of his income, he said, came from cabinet-making. He said that he had also once kept 'an eating house' at St George's Street.

In another attempt to discredit him, it was put to Smith that he had been in court before. He said that he was never in that particular court, but he had been at the Old Bailey before as a prisoner. It was eleven or twelve years earlier when he was around eighteen years of age. He said it was for receiving a stolen watch and that he got a sentence of twelve months for it: '... there was a fight at a public house, between two men, and the watch was laid on the mantelpiece, the waiter got possessed of it, and showed it to me, and wanted me to buy it, I gave him 4*l*. for it – he owed me 2*l*., and I gave him 2*l*. more ...'[3] Smith admitted that, in 1854, he had also 'passed through' the insolvency court.

He was asked about the love triangle that existed between Agar, Humphries and Emily Campbell. Bill Humphries, he said, was a house-agent and auctioneer. He also knew Emily well and said that she had 'passed as Mrs Humphries'.[4] He claimed to be so close to them that he had dined at their table with them. He had since heard, he said, that Agar was living with Emily under the name of Adams. But, according to him, Humphries never mentioned this to him. Smith was aware that she was not at home any more, but at the time he thought she had gone away to look after her ill mother.

The nature of Smith's own relationship with Humphries was also examined, and there were strong hints that it was based on criminality. An assault that took place at Bagnigge Wells was mentioned to him, but he denied any involvement in it. He said that he had read about it and he knew that 'it was about breaking into a house in Ormond Street' in order to take a child, but he said that he was not involved and had never been in that house.[5] He also denied that he had called himself the 'Rev Dr Scholfield' in order to gain entrance to the house. He said that he was not given 'a broad brimmed hat' by Humphries for the occasion nor had his face 'blackened for the purpose of not being seen'.[6] The defence also mentioned a number of other rather shady characters with whom he was acquainted, and insinuated that he was being paid by Humphries to bring these accusations against Agar. Smith did his best to defend his reputation and stuck to his story about Agar.

The man on whose account the forged cheque was to be drawn, John Deverell, was also called as a witness. As it happened he was a magistrate in Hampshire and he testified that neither the cheque nor the signature on it was his: '... this cheque is not my writing, nor signed by my authority ... I never signed a cheque for 700*l*., or authorised it – the transaction is a false one, as well as the signature – I have not the slightest idea how the prisoner could have got at my signature.'[7] He was amazed, though by the quality of the forgery, especially his signature: '... it is a very fearful representation of it – I think it has been done by tracing paper against a window....'[8]

Richard Mullens was called to give evidence himself regarding the operation he had mounted in order to capture Agar. He outlined for the court the details of what had taken place on the day that Agar was arrested. Eliza Bailey, who worked for Humphries, gave evidence stating that Agar was frequently at the house, in conversation with Smith: '... I have seen him and Smith in conversation together at various times, and have seen them drink together, and have meals together.'[9] She too knew him as 'Mr Jenkins'. The woman whom she knew as her mistress and whom she called 'Mrs Humphries', was really, she believed, Miss Campbell.

Henry Goddard told the court about his experience of what had happened on the day that Agar was apprehended. He also, for the first time, officially identified the second man on the street that day as William Pierce.[10] Goddard's colleague on the day, Jonathan Thorogood, also outlined his experiences of the day. The City of London Police officer, John Forrester, did the same. He also testified that his inquiries had shown Emily Campbell to be living with Agar at 7 Stanley Place, Paddington. They were known to their neighbours there, he told the court, as Mr and Mrs Adams.

No doubt much of Smith's story did not have the ring of truth to it. He was not the innocent party that he was trying to portray himself to be. He was far from being a model, law-abiding citizen. It is also clear that Humphries was heavily involved in Smith's actions. His sudden appearance at the public house on the day in question showed that. There is little doubt that Humphries was eager for revenge against Agar for running off with Emily. Agar was using Smith to cash forged cheques and engage in other illegal activities, but Smith was happy to do all this until Humphries found out about it. Humphries probably saw Smith's involvement with Agar as a way to get revenge, so he persuaded Smith to betray Agar.

Nevertheless, no matter how crooked Smith and Humphries were, it was clear to the jury that Agar was guilty. It did not help his cause that the prosecution was able to produce those copper-plates that he used for forging and over a hundred blank cheques from various banking institutions in evidence.[11] Some of these cheques were not forgeries, but genuine ones stolen from burgled premises. It was clear to the authorities that they had caught one of the leading crime figures in London and, in particular, a major perpetrator of forgery and fraud in the city. They did not really care what the personal motives of Smith or Humphries were, as long as they got their man. They wanted to make an example and, consequently, when Agar was found guilty he received the rather stiff sentence of transportation to Australia for life.

On this occasion the authorities were unable to punish Agar's accomplice, Pierce, mainly because they could not find him. They did indict him but, even though a reward of £50 was offered, they failed to arrest him.[12] Goddard mentioned this fact in his testimony given at Agar's trial: 'I have endeavoured to take him [i.e. Pierce] into custody on this charge – I have not been able to trace him at all, not beyond his place of residence, at Kilburn....'[13]

In Edward Agar the authorities had caught one of the major figures in London crime, but they did not as yet know the full extent of his criminal accomplishments. The court case regarding the forged cheque would not represent the last entry that British criminal history would record of Edward Agar.

As he was now facing transportation from England for life, Agar, in a rare act of compassion and loyalty, wanted to leave his beloved Fanny and his son well provided for. In order to arrange this, who else would he turn to but his trusted accomplice, William Pierce? Pierce was now in possession of most of Agar's personal store of money, so he asked him to use this to see that Fanny and the child were provided for. Had this plan worked, no more might ever have been heard of Edward Agar in England nor, in fact, of the Great Train Robbery. But relations between Pierce and Fanny did not go well and that was to have far-reaching implications. Fanny and the child lived with Pierce and his wife for a while, but she soon found that the money promised to her by Agar was slow in coming and she confronted Pierce directly on the matter: 'Agar said that Pierce was to give me the money,' she said, 'and I told Pierce so.'

The problem was that Pierce refused to act honourably and, now that Agar was out of the way, he refused to hand over any money to Fanny. 'Pierce told me he had no money,' she said. But Fanny Kay was not anyone's fool. She and Pierce had a bitter row about the matter and she took her child and left his house. That meant, however, that she soon found herself in even worse financial circumstances. Fanny now had a desire for revenge and she was in possession of information that could cause serious trouble for Pierce and a number of other people. As Agar was about to be transported for life and Fanny felt that she had nothing further to lose, she would prove to be a dangerous adversary.

Fanny Kay went straight to the governor of Newgate Prison and made the startling revelation that she had important information to impart regarding the Great Train Robbery of 1855. She told the governor that she believed Agar and Pierce to be the perpetrators of that infamous crime. She admitted that she could not tell him everything, but she assured him that Agar would be able to help him fill in the details. The amazed governor was convinced enough of her story to send her directly to the South Eastern Railway Company. She called at the office of the company secretary, Samuel Smiles, who, being busy at the time, sent her to John Rees's office. Smiles had no reason to think that this young woman would be any different to the many other reward seekers who had arrived at his office before.[14] But then, having interviewed her, Rees told him otherwise.[15] Rees was convinced enough to travel to Portland to meet Agar, who was just about to be shipped to Australia. Agar, infuriated about what Pierce had done to his beloved Fanny and Edward junior, decided to tell his amazing story.

CHAPTER 7

An Original but Criminal Idea

The story of the Great Train Robbery really began in the
1840s, when Pierce worked as a ticket printer for the South
Eastern Railway Company. His work colleagues may have
thought that they knew all about their friendly forty-year-old
colleague, who spoke with a Lancashire accent and sometimes
walked with a limp due to lumbago, but in reality they knew
very little about him.[1] On the surface he appeared to be an ordinary married man whose wife once ran a lodging house in
'Cooper's Road, Old Kent Road'.[2] The job of ticket printer may
have been an honest if not prestigious position of employment,
but Pierce's mind was always elsewhere. What his workmates
did not realize was that this man's principal occupation had
always been as a career criminal. It was while engaged at the
ticket office that he conceived of an audacious and original
robbery; his target was one of the consignments of gold and
other valuables that he saw being regularly transported, by
train and ship, from London to Paris.

Pierce knew that these consignments were loaded onto the
trains at London Bridge station in iron safes and transported to
Folkestone from where they went on the steamer to Boulogne.
He regarded his specialist inside knowledge of this process as an
opportunity not to be spurned. Most of the gold was transported by the so-called tidal train and only consignments that
arrived too late for this train were put on the mail train. It was
the mail train that Pierce wanted to target because it stopped at

the upper station in Folkestone and did not go straight through to the harbour station as the tidal train did. This would facilitate an easier getaway.

Pierce was an experienced thief and he was well aware that this would be no easy robbery to carry out successfully. After all, a theft like this from a train in transit had never been accomplished before. He knew that he would require a small group of reliable people working alongside him. With this in mind there was no better person with whom to discuss the idea than his fellow career criminal, Edward Agar. Pierce and Agar had already successfully accomplished many crimes together. Apart from the instances of cheque fraud, they had also carried out at least one robbery from a railway company managing to steal cash from an iron safe in the basement of a station. On that occasion they used duplicate keys that Agar had made from impressions of the originals obtained by Pierce.[3]

Agar, however, did not prove to be an enthusiastic accomplice from the beginning. He was doubtful about Pierce's idea, believing it to be 'not ... practicable'.[4] For him there seemed an inordinate amount of risk involved. At the time he was doing very well indeed from his cheque forgery scams and other criminal activities, and he was not keen to jeopardize all that by taking part in such a daring raid. Shortly after their discussion Agar went off on one of his frequent trips abroad, probably in order to launder corrupt money, and the plan to rob the train was shelved for the time being.

By the summer of 1854 Agar was back in England and Pierce's audacious train robbery idea was back on the agenda once again. Agar met Pierce one day in King Street, Covent Garden, apparently by accident, and in the course of their conversation Pierce brought up the idea again and asked Agar if he had given the matter any more consideration. It soon became clear that Agar was still not terribly keen on it. In any event, he told Pierce that it would be impossible to accomplish without acquiring copies of the keys to the Chubb locks that were fitted on the safes.[5] Agar believed that there was no other way to open them. They had several meetings after that when 'the conversation was generally [about] how to obtain possession of these keys'.[6] Finally Pierce managed to persuade Agar to take part by assuring him that he would find a way to get copies of the keys. On that basis they agreed to proceed and the two men set about planning the crime with their customary care and ingenuity.

No matter what Pierce had promised, the problem of getting possession of the keys to the safes would be no small issue. It was a problem exacerbated by the fact that Pierce no longer held his position of employment at the ticket office of the South Eastern Railway. He had been dismissed from there in 1850, having been caught running his own private enterprise in the printing and selling of counterfeit train tickets. His deception on that occasion was only discovered by accident. One morning, as it happened, a clerk in the superintendent's office inadvertently opened a letter that was intended for Pierce. The man was surprised to find that it was from an employee of the London and North Western Railway at Euston station, asking if Pierce would print a set of First Class tickets for him. The letter included the details of where and when he would pick up these illegal tickets. The clerk brought the letter straight to Mr Finnigan, the superintendent of the South Eastern Railway, an investigation was instigated and Pierce was duly dismissed from his post.[7]

Pierce's latest legitimate 'cover' consisted of working at Clipstone's betting office in King Street, Covent Garden, but he had much grander ambitions.

Pierce knew that it was essential that they have help from inside the South Eastern Railway if they were to pull off the train job successfully, so he set about enlisting two accomplices. In the beginning James Burgess, the train guard, was not keen to get involved in the robbery but, according to Agar, 'Pierce overtalked him into it'.[8] Both Pierce and Agar knew him well and were aware that his position as a guard would be invaluable for the job. Burgess was in his mid-thirties, married, from New Cross, with black hair and dark brown eyes; the scar on his neck was not the result of violence associated with criminality, but was instead a legacy from his former livelihood as a carpenter. In fact, Burgess was no criminal and had an unblemished record with the South Eastern Railway Company. His father was also a respectable employee of the company. In the end though, it seems that he was corrupted by Pierce's lure of money.

The other insider recruited by Pierce was William George Tester, a young clerk who had been with the South Eastern Railway Company for over eight years.[9] He was twenty-five years of age, five feet ten inches tall, with a sallow complexion, dark brown hair, dark hazel eyes and an impressive moustache and whiskers.[10] Again, he was no criminal, but his desire for money, which may have led to his involvement in this act of serious crime, was perhaps demonstrated by his interest in fashionable clothes.[11] Perhaps his need for money was exacerbated by the fact that he had only recently got married.

Pierce arranged for Agar to have a number of meetings with Burgess and Tester in various London public houses, including the Green Man in Tooley Street, the White Hart near London Bridge and the Marquis of Granby on the Lewisham Road. Pierce told Agar that Tester would show him the cash box at Margate station as an example of the type of secure boxes that were used by the railway. Agar went down and stayed in Margate overnight. Tester showed him an iron safe that was in the Margate office and the following morning a cash box that was used to transport small amounts of money on the trains. Agar listened patiently, but when Tester asked him if seeing these items would be of any help to him in making the copies of the keys to the safes, Agar told him honestly 'not the least'.[12] But when Tester told him that when he was clerk at the harbour office at Folkestone he had the keys to the safes in his possession, this seemed to suggest to Agar a far more fruitful avenue of inquiry. When he returned from Margate, Agar told Pierce: '... the only thing would be to go down to Folkestone, take an apartment and stop there and watch the tidal trains in and out, and see if the keys were there....'

So, in May 1854, about a year before the train robbery actually took place, that is exactly what Pierce and Agar did. They planned a fortnight in Folkestone where, posing as holiday-makers, they could observe and time all the activities concerned with the arrival and departure of the trains and steamboats. They booked two bedrooms and a sitting-room at a lodging-house run by a Mr and Mrs Hooker, at 27 Victoria Terrace, situated 'on the right hand side going up from the station towards the town'.[13] Running the lodging-house was only a sideline for Mr Hooker, his main occupation being that of a 'fly driver'.[14] They made the booking under Agar's favoured alias of 'Adams'. Their cover as holidaymakers allowed them to take leisurely daily walks down to Folkestone harbour to watch what was going on there. Of course their host, Mrs Harriet Hooker, did not think that this was in any way unusual. In fact, she said: '... we generally find lodgers go out after breakfast for the sea air'.[15]

Their regular visits to the harbour did arouse the suspicions of someone else, however: Inspector G.D. Hazel of the South Eastern Railway police at Folkestone saw the two men on the pier and recognized Pierce from his time working for the railway. The man in Pierce's company he did not recognize. Hazel was an experienced policeman, having worked with the Metropolitan Police for eight years before joining the South Eastern Railway, and his instincts told him that something suspicious was going on. The first time he saw the two men the tidal train had come in and they were standing close to where the passengers were boarding the steamboat. Something about their actions attracted his trained eye. He observed them carefully as they stood there for ten or fifteen minutes watching the luggage being loaded onto the boat. Then, as soon as the boat sailed for Boulogne, they walked off in the direction of the town.[16] Hazel did not follow them on that occasion, but he did inquire of Stephen Jones, one of the train guards on duty that day, whether he knew the identity of the man with Pierce. Jones told him that he did not.

After that, Hazel saw the two men together at Folkestone Harbour a further ten or twelve times, usually standing on the pier at the time of the departure or arrival of the boat to or from Boulogne. This made him suspicious enough to bring it to the attention of James Steer, superintendent of the Folkestone Police. Mr Steer and one of his men came down to the harbour and Hazel pointed the suspects out. Steer observed them himself a number of times after that. He saw them first on the harbour between ten and eleven o'clock. On one occasion he thought that they noticed him and walked off in different directions. Later that same day he saw them walking together on the road between Hythe and Folkestone.

It was Agar who first noticed the special attention the police were giving them and he realized that they were particularly interested in Pierce. It was decided that the best option would be for Pierce to leave Folkestone that very day, while Agar would stay on for a further week. Agar knew that it would be easier for him to evade the attention of the police alone. Pierce left on 9 May, telling Mrs Hooker that he had been called back to London on business.[17] The police did not give up in the absence of Pierce. Steer had a man in plain clothes follow Agar for three days, but he found nothing interesting to report.[18]

The time spent in Folkestone did not turn out to be a great success for Pierce and Agar. Agar watched all the activities he could concerning the safes, but his main interest was in how to open them and he only managed to actually see that procedure being carried out once. On that particular occasion one of the safes was being brought up to London empty. Agar watched with great interest as it was placed on the platform in full view of him. Then one of the clerks, a man he later found out was called Thomas Sharman, came out and locked it. Agar noticed that he locked only one of the two locks, using one key from a set of two hanging on a loop.[19] Agar then followed Sharman into the ticket office and watched him put the keys into a drawer.

Agar found out that Charles Chapman and Thomas Ledger were two other clerks who worked for the South Eastern

Railway in Folkestone. He discovered that these two gentlemen frequented a local public house in the upper part of the town.[20] He determined that it might be beneficial to get on friendly terms with these men so he too visited the inn with the intention of striking up a casual acquaintance with them. But, although Agar drank with them late into the evening and even allowed them to beat him at games of billiards, in the end it was all of no use. 'I did not succeed in getting any information from them,' he said, 'they gave me no facility whatever in the object I had in view.'[21]

Agar was forced to return to London frustrated. He went to Pierce's lodgings at Walnut Tree Walk, Lambeth, to give him a full report on what had happened after his departure from Folkestone. Always keen to outdo the police, and even in the midst of their frustration, they found it amusing that the police were still obviously looking for Pierce some days after his departure.[22]

Agar now wanted to try a new angle. Despite his failure with Chapman and Ledger, he came to the conclusion that he might be able to obtain copies of the keys if he was introduced personally to Sharman. Therefore, it was arranged by Pierce that Tester would bring Agar around the station at Folkestone and introduce him to Sharman as an old friend. Tester and Sharman knew each other, not terribly well, but well enough to be on friendly speaking terms. Sharman was aware that Tester was an employee of the railway based in the superintendent's office at London Bridge station and so would trust him on that basis.

Therefore, six or eight months before the robbery, Agar was back in Folkestone again, staying at the Royal Pavilion Hotel for two or three days. It was supposed to look as if Tester had met his old friend, Agar, in Folkestone by accident and had offered to show him around the station and harbour. With this in mind the two men met at the upper station on Sunday and walked together to the harbour. Tester brought Agar into the office at the harbour and began showing him around. When they saw Sharman, Tester introduced Agar as 'a friend ... stopping here for some little time.'[23] Tester then proposed that they go to the

Royal Pavilion for a glass of wine. Sharman agreed and he, a friend of his called Mr Greenstead, Tester and Agar all went together to the hotel.

As Agar plied the men with sherry and biscuits, Tester discussed work with them, touching upon such topics as how busy they were in Folkestone at that particular time of year and the amount of gold crossing the Channel. When Sharman left the hotel later that night, Tester and Agar stayed behind and, as he left, he heard them order dinner. Agar's plan was to hang around Folkestone long enough to become sufficiently friendly with Sharman so that he could spend some time with him at work and, while the man was engaged in his job, somehow get a wax impression made of the keys to the safes. Once again, however, events did not progress as Agar wanted and he was frustrated in his aims; he failed to get on friendly terms with Sharman and, in fact, found the man's personality to be quite impenetrable: 'I generally endeavoured to throw myself in the way of Sharman, but he was a very sedate young man. I did not see anything more of the chest, or the place where the keys were kept ... I could not get [in] any way familiar with Sharman....'[24]

After this failed dalliance with the 'sedate' Sharman, Agar returned to London once again with little hope of success. He and Pierce decided that they had no option now but to delay matters for a while, until they could figure out some way of getting access to the keys.

CHAPTER 8

The Intervention of Luck

Just when it seemed as if it might be impossible to proceed with the robbery, luck intervened to revive the gang's hope of success. Firstly, Tester was promoted and transferred to the London office of the South Eastern Railway Company at London Bridge station, where all matters pertaining to railway security were dealt with, including the drawing up of the guards' work roster. The second lucky incident occurred when one of the keys to the safes was lost. Captain Mold of the steamboat company had managed to lose the key, a mishap deemed serious enough for him to be forced to leave the company shortly afterwards. This meant that alterations had to be carried out to one of the locks on the safes, the three existing keys for that lock altered and one new key made to replace the lost one. Tester, in his new position with the railway, would have access to that key, at least for a short time.

The South Eastern Railway Company sent a number of letters to the Chubb lock company regarding the necessary repairs to be carried out to the safes. In July 1854, a letter from G.W. Brown, Superintendent, South Eastern Railway, to Messrs Chubb requested a meeting, at their earliest convenience, regarding the safes.[1] In August, a letter from Brown asked that three of the keys be altered and a new one made 'with all possible dispatch'.[2] The postscript to one of the letters read: 'Let all these keys come to my office when altered.'[3] Amazingly, Tester could not have been in a better position to know what was going on in respect of the safes because, as it happened, every one of these letters was written by him in the course of his work and merely signed by his superior, Brown. Tester wrote to Pierce informing him of this fortuitous development and asking him for some wax with which to make an impression of the new key when it was delivered. When Agar was told of the plan he objected, saying that he alone had the necessary skill to make such an impression. It was then decided that Tester would have to smuggle the new key out of the office for a short time in order for Agar to make the impression himself. With this in mind, as the time approached for the delivery of the key, Agar and Tester began meeting daily at the arcade near London Bridge station. They met there for two or three days but the key had not yet been delivered by Chubb's. Agar then told Tester that he 'did not like standing under the arcade so much', as it was too public, and so they agreed to meet instead at the beerhouse on the corner of Tooley Street.

By 21 October, Chubb's work on the safes was complete. Pierce and Agar were both in attendance at the beerhouse on the day that Tester finally arrived with the new key in his possession. Agar got permission from the waiting staff to go upstairs in order to wash his hands. The chambermaid led him to a bedroom and he gave her sixpence.[4] While in there, he made a wax impression of the key. Agar then came back downstairs and handed the key back to Tester, who returned it to the office.

They now, at last, had the means to make a duplicate of one of the keys to the safes. Although it seemed from their observations that one of the locks was rarely, if ever, used, they could not be sure which lock would be used or whether the practice would change if a really valuable consignment of gold was being transported. As Agar told Burgess: 'that was half way, but the one was very little use without the other....'[5] There was no escaping the fact: they would need copies of both keys and they had yet to come up with a plan to get the other one.

In order to get an impression of that second key, Pierce and Agar decided that their best option was to target Folkestone once again. Therefore, in October 1854, Agar went there again and booked in to the Royal Pavilion Hotel. This time they had devised a plan that was simple and direct, inspired by their previous observations of the office there. Firstly, Pierce sent a letter to Folkestone addressed to a 'Mr ER Archer', stating that he was sending him a small package 'in the care of either Ledger or Chapman'. That package would be insured at London Bridge station to the value of £300, which meant that it would be transported in the safe.[6] The letter arrived in Folkestone on Saturday and Agar, identifying himself as Mr Archer, collected it. Only Chapman was in the office that day; Ledger was actually away getting married.[7] Agar showed Chapman the contents of the letter from Pierce and asked if his package had arrived. Chapman remembered Agar from his earlier visits to Folkestone, but was never aware of his name. When Chapman told him that his package had not arrived, Agar informed him that he could be contacted at the Royal Pavilion as soon as it did. Meanwhile, Pierce had sent the package by rail and it was on its way to Folkestone, addressed to 'Mr ER Archer, Pavilion Hotel'.

On the following day, Sunday 30 October 1854, Agar went to the upper station 'to see the train arrive and the iron chest put out … in the ordinary way'.[8] The chest was then brought down to the lower station and Agar followed it. He called in to see Chapman once again to inquire about his package. This time it had arrived and he watched carefully as Chapman opened the safe to remove it. Once again only one lock was in use: '… he only used one key – there were two locks on the safe; but by unlocking one the safe opened, there was only one key used at that time – I noticed that he took that key from a cupboard at the back of the office, on the left hand going in.' Chapman would later remember this transaction:

'… the parcel had come, and I delivered it to him. I got it by opening the iron safe with the keys that were in my possession, which I took from the bullion room, a large closet, which was fastened by another key. I carried that key with me. I opened the closet with the key I had, took out the keys of the chest, and gave him the parcel ... The cupboard where the keys are kept is on the ground floor ... While I had charge of the keys, I kept them in the bullion-room; when I left the office, I locked them up and carried the bullion room key in my pocket. I am not aware that I ever left without taking that precaution ... Ledger had the key immediately on his return from his wedding trip. I only had it for a week or thereabouts.'[9]

Chapman then told Agar that he must fill in, and sign, a receipt before he could take possession of his package. Agar was much too experienced a forger to provide a sample of his handwriting, which might be used as evidence against him later, so he told Chapman that he could not write as he had hurt his finger. He drew Chapman's attention to two of his fingers, which he had wrapped in silk to give the impression of injury. Chapman duly filled out the form for him and Agar signed it in the name of 'E R Archer'. He then left with his package and went back to the hotel, where he asked a porter for a knife with which to open it and removed the gold sovereigns that were inside.

Agar did not realize it but Inspector Hazel was watching him again. Hazel recognized him from his previous visit to the town and still 'did not like the look of him'.[10] Hazel saw him going into the booking-office at the harbour and followed him in. He saw Agar apparently watching Sharman as he was counting money in the inner office. He saw him going to the doorway in the outer office where he was able to see Sharman by looking around the corner into the inner office. He noted that Agar was in the office for about ten or fifteen minutes but brought nothing out. Hazel later discovered from Sharman that Agar, on that particular occasion, had been asking about his package. Hazel warned Sharman that he regarded Agar as 'a suspicious character', but Sharman was not convinced.[11] He even told the inspector that he thought he was wrong about Agar. Although he believed that Agar was acting suspiciously, Hazel did not have a sufficiently strong reason to take legal action against him.[12] The following day Hazel saw Agar again. This time he was on the pier, between eleven and twelve o'clock, as the boat was getting ready to start for Boulogne. Then Tester arrived and Hazel saw them walk off together in the direction of the Royal Pavilion. They were, Hazel noticed, 'very friendly'. Later that day the inspector saw Tester at Folkestone Harbour station. He watched him leave for London on the seven o'clock train. Tester and Agar had looked to be on such friendly terms that he decided not to say anything to Tester regarding his suspicions of Agar.[13]

Superintendent Steer had also seen Agar again. He noticed him opposite the Royal Pavilion on Folkestone Harbour, standing under an umbrella in the rain with a tall gentleman, whom he could not see properly. Once again they seemed to walk off when they saw him coming: the tall man went into the Hotel and Agar made off in the direction of the town.

Now that they were sure where the keys were kept in the office, Pierce and Agar made another trip about a week later, to Dover this time, and checked into the Rose Inn 'just by the market house, opposite the church'.[14] They took a walk 'over the hills to Folkestone ... by the sea coast' and watched the arrival of the boat from Boulogne. It was a fine warm day.[15] They walked down to the harbour and positioned themselves so that they could keep a covert watch on the only door to the harbour office, which faced the sea. They saw Chapman and Ledger leave the office unattended as they went to meet the arriving boat from Boulogne. Pierce and Agar then went up to the door of the office, which they found was 'on the latch, not locked'.[16] Agar stayed at the door as Pierce slipped inside. Acting according to the directions given to him by Agar, Pierce went straight to the relevant cupboard, removed the key from its drawer and brought it out to Agar. As soon as Agar had taken a wax impression of it, Pierce returned the key to the cupboard and the two men left completely unobserved. They walked back to Dover where they had tea at the Rose before returning to London by train. It was as simple as that.

Agar met Burgess in London to inform him about the success they had had in acquiring the second key. Burgess lived at New Cross at that time, and they met near there at the Marquis of Granby public house on the Lewisham Road, where they had all met previously on a number of occasions. Burgess was delighted with the progress they had made with the keys and, according to Agar, said: 'It is a good job, and I will do my best to assist you.'[17] His role would be crucial to the whole plan.

As Agar now had both his wax impressions, the next step for him was to set about making some duplicate keys. As he was in the middle of a serious row with Fanny around that time, he decided to move out of their lodgings at 13 Harleyford Road, Vauxhall, where they had been living as husband and wife under the names of Mr and Mrs Adams. They rented the place from a Mr and Mrs James and Mary Ann Porter and had lived there for about seven weeks in all.[18] Pierce was a frequent visitor to their lodgings, although Mrs Porter only ever knew him as Mr Peckham. According to Mrs Porter, he visited about twice the first week that Agar and Fanny moved in and afterwards more frequently.

Agar had to begin working on the keys in an empty room over the gateway at Pierce's house at Walnut Tree Walk using blank keys, files, a hammer and a chisel. He worked there until he and Fanny made up the 'altercation' between them and moved together to Cambridge Villas in December 1854. Mr and Mrs 'Adams', as they continued to call themselves, moved into their new home the week before Christmas. Pierce helped them to move their furniture in a rented cart. He also came frequently to Cambridge Villas to help Agar with the keys. He assisted in the making of a file and did 'any little thing ... [that Agar] wanted him to do....'[19] Most of the work took place 'in the wash-house adjoining the garden'.[20] The tools were kept in 'a wooden box painted green and also in a small wainscot box'.[21]

Once Agar was satisfied that his duplicate keys were as accurate as he could make them from the wax impressions, the next step was to try them out on the actual locks of the safes and refine them if necessary. This is where Burgess came in. A number of times when he had the safes on his train, Agar joined him. Somewhere on the line, he would sneak into Burgess's van in order to test and alter the keys while the train was in transit: 'I travelled by the train as a second or a first class passenger, and ... I used to get into the van and try the keys, at Reigate, or any other place....'[22] He had some difficulties, he recalled. 'The keys would not open the safe at first, they would go in but would not open it.'[23] Eventually, though, he got them to work: 'I tried them five or six times, and altered them if they did not fit, and they at last opened it.'[24] If any stranger happened to ask him why he was travelling on the train, he would identify himself as 'a commercial traveller'. It was a cover he also used at any hotel at which he stayed.

When the keys were ready, they all met at Burgess's home to work out the final details of the job, including which train to attempt and how to sell the valuables afterwards. The amount of planning and effort that they had put into their criminal scheme so far, and the considerable risk involved in it, necessitated a substantial reward, so they decided not to act until a sufficiently valuable haul of gold was being transported. For their plan to succeed it was essential that Burgess was on duty on the mail train when the next substantial cargo of valuables was being transported. In order to ensure this, Tester altered the guards' work roster. Burgess was scheduled to work on the 8.30 p.m. mail train and the Second Class return from Dover in April so, in order to prolong this, Tester simply added the words 'and May' to the roster. This meant that all staff would be assigned to the same trains in May as they were in April. John Peake Knight, the 'out of door' superintendent for the South Eastern Railway, noticed this alteration and mentioned it to Tester. According to him, 'it was irregular to continue the guards for two months together' but Tester replied simply 'that it was of no consequence, that it had been done before....'[25]

Another important issue to be dealt with was the weight of the gold. They were aware that the boxes containing the gold would be weighed a number of times en route and those weights would be compared to the ones recorded at London Bridge station before departure. If the boxes were found to be too light, the alarm would be raised and they might not have sufficient time to escape. In order to get around this, they decided to replace the gold with lead shot. In order to work out how much lead shot they would need, they based their calculations on the weight of around £12,000 worth of gold, because they decided that that would be as much as Agar and Pierce would be able to carry. They 'calculated that the 12,000L worth of gold would weigh about two cwt'.[26]

In order to get the required amount of lead shot, Agar went with Pierce to the shot-tower on the Surrey side of Hungerford Bridge, where it was manufactured. Agar stayed outside as Pierce went in and bought one hundredweight of lead shot, which he placed in two carpet-bags. He brought these out to the gate and Agar helped him to carry them. They walked across the suspension bridge and caught an omnibus to Cambridge Villas. Pierce went back to the shot-tower on two more occasions and bought 50 lb of lead each time, making two half hundred-weights.[27] Agar did not accompany Pierce on the second or third occasions. They were now satisfied that they had an amount of lead shot equivalent to the weight of £12,000 in gold, to take the place of the gold in the wooden boxes.

At Cambridge Villas, Agar and Pierce first placed the bags of lead in the parlour and then afterwards in Agar's trunk up in the first floor bedroom where he and Fanny slept. Later they moved the lead to the wash-house in the backyard, where they weighed it out into 8 lb and 4 lb parcels. These amounts were placed inside 'blue check bags' that they had made themselves from material bought at Shoolbred's on Tottenham Court Road.[28] These were then stored inside a box.

Fanny Kay, Edward junior and a servant, Charlotte Paynter, were all living in the house with Agar at that time. It was a two storey house with two rooms on the ground floor and three on the first floor. If Fanny had wanted to see what was hidden in the box she could have done so as it was not locked but this, Agar said later, did not worry him as he knew that she did not have 'curiosity enough to do so'.[29] The real truth was that she was well used to his criminal activities and very accustomed to suspicious items being stashed around the house. She had learned, through experience, that when you lived with a man like Agar it was better not to ask too many questions. When they had measured out all the lead shot into the small bags, they had ten or twenty pounds left over. They did not want to leave this incriminating material around the house, so Agar and Pierce carried it out in their pockets and 'distributed it, in the fields, and the road, in the neighbourhood of Pierce's house....'[30]

They bought four courier bags made 'of drab leather' with 'a strap to sling over the shoulder and go under the arm'. These bags were ideal because they could be 'easily concealed by a cloak or a cape' yet were very strong.[31] Pierce and Agar designed them to their own precise requirements and drew the pattern on a board. They were then made up for them by a 'leathersellers' on the corner of Drury Lane and Queen Street.[32] As soon as they collected the bags, they began testing them. They carried the shot in them but soon found that 'a few of the stitches came undone' and Agar had to make some wax ends and sew them up himself.[33] As it was agreed that Tester would come down to Reigate on the night of the robbery and take some of the gold back to London with him in order to lighten the load on Agar and Pierce, a special bag had to be provided for him as well. This one Agar made himself. It was simple, black and made of leather.

They decided to move the lead shot to Pierce's house in Crown Terrace. For this purpose the courier bags were filled with the lead and then placed inside the larger carpet-bags. Tester's bag was also placed inside the carpet-bags. Pierce got a horse and cart for this job. Finally, all their preparations were at an end and the gang was ready to attempt the first train robbery in history.

CHAPTER 9

The First Train Robbery in History

———————

E ven with inside information the gang could not be exactly sure when a suitably large shipment of gold was going to be made, so Agar and Pierce began making the journey to London Bridge station on successive evenings, each time totally prepared to initiate their plan. They travelled with one carpet-bag each, filled with hay and some lead shot; the rest of the shot was inside the four courier bags, carried two each by straps over their shoulders, close to their bodies and hidden under their cloaks.[1] The small leather bag for Tester was inside the larger bags. They made this journey to the station about five times without success. Most evenings they hired a cab either at the stand in Chalk Farm or at a public house called 'The Mother Red Cap'. Pierce was disguised with 'a cloak, a black wig, fake whiskers and a broad brimmed hat'.[2] His wig was probably the one 'dressed' for him by John Honnor, his neighbour at Walnut Tree Walk, who had known Pierce for four or five years.'[3] Along with the lead shot, Agar also had the extra weight of a mallet, a chisel and some wax and tapers, needed to open and reseal the wooden boxes. Each night the cab took them to St Thomas Street, Agar would get out, walk into London Bridge station and find out from Tester or Burgess whether a suitable shipment of gold was being transported on the mail train that night. If it was, they had organized a signal. On most of those evenings at the station Agar met Tester; only once did he meet Burgess. When they all knew that the job was not going ahead on a particular night, Tester usually came to the cab and had a conversation with Pierce. Then Agar and Pierce would return to the neighbourhood of Crown Terrace to await the following evening.

On Tuesday 15 May 1855, Pierce and Agar walked to 'a coffee-house in High Street, Camden Town, near the Southampton Arms' and the Turnpike Gate.[4] They had some tea and then Pierce left Agar there with the bags, while he went out to hail a cab. They drove to St Thomas Street, where Agar got out as usual and went into London Bridge station. Agar saw Burgess at the station gate used by the carriages. Burgess lifted his cap and wiped his face, which was the signal that the job was going ahead.[5] Burgess knew that the consignments from the three London firms of Abel, Spielmann and Bult were about to be transported on his train that evening and it was a large enough haul to serve their purpose. Once he had given Agar the signal, Burgess went back to work on his train.

Agar walked back to St Thomas Street where Pierce was waiting in the cab. He climbed in and told Pierce that the job was on. He instructed the driver to take them to the station. As the cab moved, they slung the courier bags over their shoulders and put on their cloaks. On arrival they took their carpet-bags from the cab and paid the driver. Tester was waiting for them 'between the outer station and the incline' and, as Agar and Pierce approached, 'in a hurried voice' said: 'All right.'[6] He then walked off towards the ticket office. Agar bought two First Class tickets. He gave the two carpet-bags to the porter, told him that they were for the Dover train, but instructed the man to wait for him. They kept the courier bags. He gave one of the tickets to Pierce and they walked together onto the platform. As Pierce got into the First Class carriage, Agar walked to Burgess's van with the porter. He saw the man hand their carpet-bags over to Burgess, and Agar again said that they 'were for Dover'.[7]

By then it was only a few minutes to departure. Pierce took his seat with the other passengers in the First Class carriage, while Agar waited on the platform and, when no one was looking, slipped through one of the small doors into Burgess's van. He hid in the corner, in a small space intended for the guard, and Burgess threw his apron over him. Burgess continued to take in items and Agar had to wait five or ten minutes in that position. He later admitted that 'the time passed very long' until the train finally started to move. Once they were moving, Agar left his hiding-place and got straight to work. He immediately set about opening the first of the two iron safes using his duplicate keys. As usual, only one of the locks was in use and his key worked perfectly.[8] The safe contained two wooden boxes, one of which he removed. This one contained Abel's gold bars. Using a pair of pincers he pulled off the iron bands that were nailed around the box and with 'box wood wedges' and 'a mallet' he broke his way into the box. It opened up 'without too much difficulty' and inside were the six bars of gold.[9] He put one of the bars in the black bag to be passed on to Tester at Reigate station, as arranged. He handed the bag to Burgess who left it in the front part of the carriage. He then placed the other bars inside one of the courier bags. He took some of the blue check bags, which contained the lead shot in weights of 4 lb and 8 lb, and placed them inside the wooden box. He then refastened the iron hoops on the box and placed it back inside the iron safe.

By the time he had done all this the train arrived at Reigate station, where it made a scheduled stop. Agar hid himself again. Tester, who had travelled down on the same train, now got out and made his way to Burgess's van. From his hiding-place Agar heard Tester say: 'Where is it? Where is it?' Burgess handed him the bag containing the bar of gold. Tester would take the next train back to London with his valuable bag. Also at Reigate, Pierce took the opportunity of leaving the First Class carriage and joining Burgess and Agar.

Once the train started moving again, they removed the other small box from the same iron safe. When Agar forced it open he found that it contained American gold coin and 'some coupons of a foreign railway', which was the property of Spielman & Co.[10] Agar removed all the contents and replaced them with the lead shot. He then screwed the lid back into place. Some seals on the outside had been broken, so Agar replaced these by melting 'a small wax taper' and using some steel seals with initials on them that they had purchased for the job. He then placed the box back inside the safe and locked the safe using his key.

Next they moved on to the second safe. Once again Agar's key worked without any problem and they found that this safe contained only one larger wooden box with 'ropes at each end for handles'.[11] They prised it open and inside were small bars of gold of a different colour, which Agar recognized to be Californian gold.[12] It was, in fact, the Californian gold that belonged to Messrs Bult & Co. They took out as many of the bars as they thought they had lead shot to replace. They put the shot in, closed the box as well as they could and replaced it in the safe. Unfortunately, the box had become damaged and could not be adequately repaired in the circumstances. Their haul of gold, coin and paper money was now safely inside the bags. They swept up the dust from the floor of the carriage and everything was done by the time the train reached Folkestone. They did not know it but, as it happened, they had failed to bring sufficient lead shot with them and one of the boxes now weighed significantly less than it had done at London Bridge station.

When the train came to a stop, with Agar and Pierce in hiding, Burgess opened the door to his van and the Folkestone staff removed the safes from the train. They would be taken to the booking-office at the harbour and stored there until the following morning and the departure of the next steamboat to Boulogne. The train then continued its journey to Dover with Agar, Pierce and Burgess on board.

Meanwhile, Tester arrived back at London Bridge station with his bar of gold and at around ten minutes past ten he went into the office of Frederick Russell, the booking clerk, for a chat. It seemed to Russell to be a fairly normal casual conversation, although he did notice that Tester 'appeared rather excited.'[13] For Tester to engage in casual conversation like this was, perhaps, strange behaviour for someone in possession of a stolen bar of gold. It would, however, have the advantage of locating him in London at the time that the gold was stolen and, also, he might have felt that engaging in normal banter in this way would put him above suspicion later on. He even told Russell that he had just been to Redhill and back.[14] Tester asked Russell if he was going home by the 10.20 p.m. train to Greenwich that night, which was the last train. Tester said that he intended to travel home on that train.

Then Tester took an even more remarkable and reckless action; he left his black bag containing the bar of gold 'in a recess against the fireplace' saying that 'he would be back in a few minutes'.[15] John Perry, the night-watchman, had left the office ten minutes earlier, but now came back in. Russell asked him to 'shift a box ... out of the way' and as he did so, Perry saw the black bag '... down against this box'.[16] It was, he thought, 'about a foot long or more'.[17] He moved it out of the way and asked Russell whose bag it was. Russell told him that it was Tester's. Perry noticed that it was 'very heavy and lumpy ... as if a stone was in it'.[18] Russell described the bag as being fifteen or eighteen inches long and '... made of black shiny leather'.[19] Russell had never seen Tester with such a bag before. This was a very risky strategy on Tester's behalf. Perhaps it was an attempt to prove that there was nothing valuable in the bag, but had Perry glanced inside it the whole game would have been up. As it happened, he did not, and seven or eight minutes later Tester returned and took it away. He joined Russell on the last train to Greenwich that evening, before going on home to Lewisham.[20]

Agar and Pierce disembarked from the train at the end of the line in Dover. They walked from the station to the Dover Castle Hotel carrying the carpet-bags in their hands and the courier bags on their shoulders. They went into the coffee room, placed their carpet-bags under a window in the corner and calmly ordered supper. The waiter, Robert Clark, asked them if they needed beds for the night and they told him that they did not, as they were catching the 2 a.m. train to London.[21] When Clark went off to get their order they took the courier bags off their shoulders and placed them in the corner with the carpet-bags. Once they had finished eating, Agar walked to the pier in Dover and, when he was sure that no one was watching, threw his tools and other items off the pier into the sea. Pierce waited patiently in the hotel for him to return. When they were ready to leave they ordered some brandy in a soda water bottle to take away and a few cigars. They paid the bill, picked up their bags and set off on foot to the station.

When they reached Dover station they simply walked through the booking-office. They did not have to buy tickets for London because Pierce had already sourced two fake London to Ostend return tickets, which bore the appropriate stamps to indicate that they had actually taken the trip. It seems that Pierce had acquired these tickets from a man called Richard Gower who was engaged in a practice with which Pierce was very familiar, that is, the selling of illegal counterfeit tickets.[22] Outside the ticket office they met Joseph Witherden, the porter, who offered to carry their bags for them. Agar refused: '… He very politely said he would carry it [but] I objected to his doing so; he offered to take it out of my hand.' Witherden inquired about their tickets and they showed him the two tickets from the Ostend line. He then grew inquisitive about their other bags, assuming that they must have some, having travelled to Ostend and back. Agar told him that they had got them through the day before. As he did so, he thrust 'a few shillings in the man's hand' and this ended their conversation.[23]

The 2 a.m. train to London was not busy that night and they had a carriage all to themselves. As they travelled along they were able to throw the hay that was inside the carpet-bags out of the train. Then, when the train stopped at one of the stations along the line, Pierce got out and dumped the now empty carpet-bags behind the door of the waiting-room.[24] A porter spoke to him but he told the man that he was merely looking for a friend.[25] He then reboarded the train. They knew that the nearer the train got to London, the greater their chances of escape.

CHAPTER 10

Back Home

———•—•———

The Dover to London train arrived at London Bridge station that morning, at around 5 a.m. As Agar and Pierce looked out the train window there was no unusual police presence, no one waiting to arrest them. They exited the train carriage as casually as they could. The door was opened for them by Matthew Dickenson, the porter, who asked them if they needed a cab. They declined. They had no luggage to collect from the guard's van so they walked down the platform with the bags on their shoulders hidden under their cloaks. Slipping past the two policemen posted at the entrance to the station, they hailed a cab for themselves and told the driver to take them to the Great Western station at Paddington. When they were near there they told the driver that he had made a mistake and that they had wanted to go to Euston station instead.[1] They got out at Euston Square and went into a public house, where they remained 'some little time' in the parlour.[2] This was all intended, of course, to throw any potential investigators off their trail.

When they left the pub Pierce hailed another cab, which brought them to the neighbourhood of Crown Terrace, but not right up to Pierce's front door. They carried their haul the rest of the way. Losing no time, having deposited the valuables in Pierce's house, they took a cab to London Bridge, taking some of the American coin with them. Agar met Tester at Borough Market and got the other bar of gold from him as arranged.

Tester then went to work, while Agar and Pierce took a cab to Leadenhall Street, 'down by the side of the East India House'.[3] Agar remained in the cab with the bar of gold while Pierce went to Messrs Massey, the goldsmiths and money-changers based at 116 Leadenhall Street at the corner of St Mary Axe Street, 'almost opposite the East India House'. By now it was between nine o'clock and half past. Pierce was dealt with by John Matthews, the manager of Messrs Massey. Pierce told Matthews that he wished to sell his American coin and Matthews agreed to give him £210 13s for it. Matthews noticed how tired this tall customer looked, as if he had been travelling.[4] When Matthews offered to pay him by cheque, Pierce insisted that he get it in gold. Matthews did not have that much gold on the premises so, with Pierce's agreement, he went off to sell the coin in the trade. Matthews first got banknotes for the coin, which he then exchanged for gold at the Bank of England. After about half an hour he returned and gave Pierce the gold.[5] When Pierce got back to the cab he told Agar that he had received 'upwards of 200L' for the coin.[6] He also explained how he had decided to wait for the gold rather than accept payment by cheque. Next the two criminals drove to 37 Haymarket, 'on the right hand side of the way going from Pall Mall, nearly at the top'.[7] Situated there was the business premises of a money-changer, Rudolf Prommell. Pierce sold Mr Prommell the rest of the American coin that they had brought with them. Prommell bought two hundred American Gold Eagles for £203 6s 8d.[8] This time Pierce did accept payment by cheque, made out on the Union Bank of London in Pall Mall East. As a consequence this transaction took no more than ten minutes. Agar then went straight to the Union Bank and had the cheque cashed by the manager, Alexander White. He received the amount in British gold sovereigns.

Agar was happy for Pierce to hold on to all the money raised from the sale of the American coin for now, as he did not, at that time, need it: 'I was not at all in want of money at that time – Pierce had no money, he was supporting himself by pledging his things, and what money I lent him; he was in destitute circumstances.' If that was true, Pierce's greater need may well have been the result of his gambling habits. It showed the good level of trust that existed between the two men at that time.

No doubt using some of the money that he had made from the sale of the American coin, Pierce hired a horse and cart in Grove Street, for them to use to transport the rest of their haul over to Agar's place at Cambridge Villas, Shepherd's Bush. Fanny was at home when they arrived. First they unloaded the cart as quickly as they could and dropped the bags in the front parlour behind the door. Then, as Pierce left to return the horse and cart to its owner, Agar moved the bags upstairs and hid them in a trunk in the bedroom. It was the same American-made trunk in which he had earlier kept the lead shot. After this, Agar did not see Pierce again for a few days.[9] The plan was that they would not meet Burgess or Tester again until it was deemed safe to do so.

The gold was safe for the moment at Agar's house in Shepherd's Bush, but they had to do something with it. They decided that the best way to dispose of it, and not get caught, was to melt the bars down to a new size. First, though, they decided to cut off a piece from one of the bars and sell it in order to raise some more funds. They took one bar of Australian gold out to the wash-house in the backyard. The windows of the wash-house had been whitened out to prevent anyone from looking inside.[10] They placed a chisel on the gold bar and began to hit it with a hammer but soon found that it was harder to cut than they had imagined. Pierce was forced to go to a toolmaker called Buck on Tottenham Court Road to purchase a heavier hammer.[11] Eventually they did manage to cut 100 ounces from the bar and Pierce sold it for £3 per ounce, netting them £300.

They would need a furnace if they were to melt the remaining gold so they set about building an improvised version in one of Agar's rooms at Cambridge Villas. Pierce went to get some fire-bricks while Agar pulled out the common stove that he had in the first floor back room. Pierce transported the bricks back to the house on a horse and cart. Once they had prepared the makeshift furnace, they purchased a number of essential items at a supplier in St John's Square, Clerkenwell, including a number of crucibles and a pair of scales and weights. Once everything was ready, they set to work. It proved to be hot, dirty and difficult. Their plan was to recast the gold into ingots of a hundred ounces each. They cut the bars, a hundred ounces off at a time, and then melted that in the furnace using a crucible. Charcoal and coke, which they purchased in St John's Street, Wilderness Row, was what they burned in the fire to attain the high temperatures required.[12] The fire was incredibly hot and once, when Agar was removing the crucible from the fire, it fractured at the place where it was being held by the tongs, sending gold scattering all over the floor and leaving a scorch mark where it fell.[13] The heat became so great at one point that they had to put the fire out 'for fear of setting fire to the chimney' and burning the house down.[14] In order to protect themselves from the heat and splashes they used cut-up courier bags as aprons.

No one came into the room while they were engaged in this work. Pierce came to work every day, only going home to sleep. They had their meals together. Fanny did hear strange noises coming from the room in which they were working. She realized that the sounds were '... like the roaring of a large fire'.[15] She also saw Pierce bringing down what she described as 'square pieces of stone' from the room upstairs, 'one end of which was in a pail and the other he held with a duster'.[16] She brought some bitter ale to the door once or twice, but when she tried to enter the room they ran to the door to prevent her from doing so. She also noticed how hot and dirty they both looked when they came down for their meals. She did ask them what they were doing up there, but the only reply she got from them was the rather unlikely one of 'leather apron weaving'. This hot and difficult work went on for most of a week until the gold was shaped into new bars that weighed about a hundred ounces each.[17] These were placed in the trunk in Agar and Fanny's bedroom.

Now the gold had to be sold. Agar had a contact who could arrange that for him. He went to his most significant criminal associate, a man who was one of the most important and least known figures in the London criminal underworld: James Townsend Saward, or 'Jim the Penman' as he was known. Saward was a crooked barrister, forger and all round rogue. He was one of the linchpins of London crime and Agar had known him for around six years. He had watched Saward at work in his official role as a legal representative at Westminster Hall and had even engaged him in his professional capacity as a barrister when Saward wrote a number of letters for him.[18] Saward led a remarkable and fantastic double life running his barrister's chambers at 4 Hare Court, Temple, and, alongside, managing a career as a leading criminal. Saward and Agar had carried out many scams together, especially forgery, a crime for which they shared a special passion. Saward had a sizeable criminal gang running his various forgery scams. With his influence and connections he was in a good position to fence stolen goods and it was in this capacity that he could be useful to Agar. In order to conduct their latest bit of business they met a number of times at a public house 'of the sign of the Alma' on Bell's Pond Road, near Dalston Turnpike.[19] According to Agar, Saward was very keen to get involved from the beginning: 'He said he had read the account of the robbery in the papers. He said, "I suppose this is part of it." I said "Yes." He then said he could get rid of the gold.'[20] In fact, Saward assured him that he could 'do it very well'.[21] A deal was struck for a considerable amount of money and the handover of the first batch was arranged.

While he was in the process of selling the gold, Agar had yet another argument with Fanny, which caused him to move out of the house at Shepherd's Bush and take an apartment on his own in Kilburn. Since he still had the remaining gold in his trunk, Pierce helped him to move. 'The gold was ... brought to my lodgings at Kilburn,' said Agar. 'Pierce and I carried it there, two or three bars at a time.'[22] Once again he rented this new accommodation under the name of Adams. Fanny remained with Edward junior at Cambridge Villas for the time being.

Perhaps in a display of nervousness about being apprehended,

in June Pierce also moved lodgings. He went from Crown
Terrace to Kilburn Villa, which was 'about half a mile nearer to
London' than Agar's lodgings. Then it was decided that Agar
should move in with him for a week or fortnight, which meant
that the gold had to be moved yet again. As they moved it, Pierce
told Agar's neighbours that he was moving to Scotland. Pierce
came up with the idea of burying the remaining gold in a hole at
his house, in Kilburn Villa. Agar agreed:

> ... he said he would make a hole for it in the pantry, and he did
> so, and the gold was buried in the hole....[23]

> [Pierce] made a hole in the pantry at the bottom of the stairs of
> his own house at Kilburn Villa, and there he buried it, under
> the steps which go into the house from the front garden, there
> is a fore court to the house – you ascend to the house by four
> or five steps – the pantry is underneath those steps, and he
> made the hole in the pantry.[24]

It was while Agar was living with Pierce that arrangements
were made for Burgess and Tester to come round for the first
division of the spoils from the robbery. The railway workers had
shown good patience, as around two months had passed since
the robbery and they had received nothing until now. Only now
did Agar and Pierce think it was safe for them all to meet. Agar,
Pierce and Tester all received £600 each, while Burgess received
£700, as had been agreed.[25] Pierce had paper currency in his
possession, part of which he had got from the Bank of England
using the assumed name of Edgington, and they were all paid
their shares in these notes rather than in gold.[26]

Tester, it seems, was wondering what he should do with his
share of the money. He knew that he could not risk being seen
to have suddenly acquired a large amount of money without a
credible explanation. Agar told him that he had £700 worth of
Spanish bonds that he was willing to sell him. He had bought
them, he said, some considerable time before the robbery,

through a Mr Young, a stockbroker based at Bartholomew Lane. He agreed to sell £500 worth of these bonds to Tester immediately. Tester accepted the deal and paid for them 'with part of the notes that he had received as his share of the division.'[27] They were payable to the bearer, transferable through a stockbroker:

> It was Tester's own proposition that he should buy the Spanish bonds – he did not know that I had Spanish bonds to sell – he asked me which was the best way for him to invest his money; I told him that Spanish bonds were paying 7 per cent, and that it was merely transferring a bit of paper, I had some that I bought ... and I would sell them to him ... he consented to do so, and took 500*l*. worth of them ... without making any further inquiry....

The evening, it seems, passed off in a very convivial fashion and they were all pleased with how things had gone. At least, that was Agar's impression of it: 'We were together for some time on the evening that the division was made – I stopped there rather late, all the buses had gone – I walked with Tester and Burgess to the cab stand by the canal bridge that runs across the Paddington Road, and they got into a cab and came into town.'[28] But Agar's subsequent arrest for forgery and the repercussions caused by it would soon bring this sense of peace and camaraderie to an end.

CHAPTER 11

Trust and Treachery

—————•—•————

As time passed, Agar, Pierce, Burgess and Tester grew ever more secure in the knowledge that they had managed to pull off one of the most sensational robberies of the century. It seemed as if the career of William Tester was going from strength to strength; in September 1855 he resigned from the South Eastern Railway Company and took up a new position as general manager of Swedish Railways. It is ironic that at the time of his departure he was given a glowing testimonial by the secretary of the South Eastern Railway Company. On 28 September 1855, over four months after the robbery, Samuel Smiles wrote to Tester:

> With reference to your request to be furnished with a testimonial from the directors upon your leaving the company's service, I am desired to express their entire satisfaction with the very efficient manner in which you have performed the duties devolving on you in the various capacities and departments through which you have passed during the period that you have been in the company's service – namely, eight years and a half; and they also desire me to add that they consider you a very suitable person for the position to which they understand you are appointed on the Royal Swedish Railway....[1]

Along with this, Tester got testimonials from the general manager, Captain R.H. Barlow, the superintendent, G.W. Brown, and the goods manager, J.C. Shaw, along with a number of others.[2] Burgess, for his part, just carried on working for the South Eastern Railway, unhindered in any way, it seems, by the authorities or by any sense of guilt. He was, no doubt, enjoying the first instalment of funds that had come from the crime.

Pierce and Agar continued, as they always had, to lead lavish lives funded by their criminal activities. After the success of the train robbery they turned their attention once again to Agar's crime of choice, the forging of cheques. Agar was now living in his new lodgings at Stanley Place, Paddington Green, with Emily Campbell. After Agar left her, Fanny remained living at Cambridge Villas for a short time until she moved into lodgings in St George's Road. Edward junior was not with her during this time, an indication of how chaotic her life was. Agar, however, always seemed to be making sure that his son was cared for. Around this time he arranged for the boy to spend some time at Rotherhithe being looked after by his cousin. Fanny had not seen Agar for some considerable time when he arrived at her lodgings in St George's Road, shortly before his arrest for forgery. Considering their past experiences, however, one has to assume that they would eventually have ended up back together had things turned out differently. The reason for this visit was once again the welfare of Edward junior. The plan now was that Pierce and his wife would look after the child for a while. Fanny agreed to this and the day before Agar's arrest she brought the child with her to a meeting with Pierce and Agar in a public house, from where Pierce left with the child in a cab.

On the day of his arrest Agar met Pierce at his lodgings in Stanley Place at two o'clock and they walked across the fields to Shepherd's Bush in order to pick up some of the child's clothes and the pram from Fanny. Pierce went to wait in a public house, while Agar went to Fanny's lodgings. Agar was unhappy when he saw that part of the child's pram had been damaged and while he was at Fanny's lodgings he wrote a letter of complaint to the nurse, intending to send it along with the part that had been damaged. He delivered the child's items to Pierce and then caught a bus around four o'clock, to get to Holborn and his appointment. According to whom you believe, that appointment was either with Bill Humphries, in order to get back from him the money that he had lent him or, as the police claimed at his trial, it was with William Smith in order to collect the money from the bank cheque scam. When he was arrested, Agar still had the letter to the nurse and the parcel containing the part from the pram in his possession.

At the time of Agar's arrest, a substantial amount of the gold from the train robbery was still left unsold. A few bars were in Agar's trunk at Pierce's house and the rest was hidden in the hole at the same address: '... at the time I was arrested my large American trunk was at Pierce's house, containing three or four bars. I left those in it for sale. The remaining portion was placed in the hole....' His share of the proceeds from the robbery – £600 in notes, along with a Spanish bond for £200 – were also inside that trunk when he was arrested.[3] He had another £3,000 in the bank, which, after his arrest, he arranged for a solicitor called Wontner to take possession of.[4] Agar always claimed that he never saw any more of the gold that Pierce had hidden in that hole: '... what became of it afterwards,' he said, 'I do not know.'[5]

As soon as he was convicted and imprisoned, Agar's primary concern became the welfare of Fanny and Edward junior. At least he could console himself with the fact that he had sufficient funds to support them. He instructed Wontner to give the money that he had in the Bank of England to Pierce so that he would invest it for Fanny and the child: 'The money was given to him with the understanding that he was to re-invest it for my child ... The money was to be disposed of for the benefit of my child and Fanny Kay.'[6] The fact that Agar did not just give the money directly to Fanny was probably an indication that he did not trust her to use it sensibly. Her liking for alcohol was the major reason for this decision. As he was in prison, he did not see Pierce in person so he contacted him through Wontner and in writing. Pierce's lack of commitment to the idea of looking after Fanny and the child was perhaps evident from the beginning: 'I expected Pierce to come to me, but he never came. He got the whole of my money in notes and £200 in gold, as well as the remaining bars which had not been disposed of when I was arrested.'[7] As Pierce had done so well out of the train robbery, Agar thought that he could trust him to use the £3,000 for the benefit of Fanny and the child. There is some irony in the fact that Agar, a man who had lived a life of crime founded on the betrayal of people's trust, was himself betrayed.

At first Fanny continued to live at St George's Road, until, in January 1856, she moved in with the Pierces. Her child was already living with them. Unfortunately, disputes over money soon developed: 'Pierce provided the money ... up to January – I cannot say how much he gave me, it was different sums; he was to have allowed me 1*l.* a week, but he did not do that.'[8] She took careful note of the things belonging to Agar that she saw around the house, perhaps with a view to selling them at some stage. She noticed two trunks containing his clothes, a box of tools and a few other items, but no money. 'I saw his watch there,' she said, 'and a set of shirt studs, and a diamond ring, but no money or notes.'[9] She stayed living with the Pierces until 'the latter part of April' when she left, according to herself, 'on account of words with Pierce' about money.[10] After she left, her need for money only grew more desperate and she was still appealing to Pierce for funds. He, however, became more and more unhelpful: '... after I left his house in April, I had no means of support, and made application to Pierce for money, I got it, and I applied again and got it, I applied to him again and was refused.'[11] With Agar in custody and about to be transported to Australia, Pierce could not bring himself to give Fanny any more money. He completely reneged on his agreement with his old accomplice. The struggle between Fanny and Pierce over the money went on for several months in 1856, until she came to the conclusion that he had double-crossed them. Pierce's betrayal led Fanny to a momentous decision; she decided to take action regarding the Great Train Robbery. This was obviously something that Pierce had never expected, if he had, perhaps he would not have acted in the way that he did. His dishonourable, arrogant and reckless action was about to have severe consequences not only for himself, but for his family and for Burgess and Tester.

Fanny paid a visit to the governor of Newgate Prison, who ironically was Mr Weatherhead, who had been the stationmaster at London Bridge station on the evening of the robbery. She told him that she knew who had carried out the Great Train Robbery of 1855. Weatherhead sent her to the South Eastern Railway where she was interviewed by John Rees. On the basis of the evidence from Fanny, even before he had interviewed Agar, Rees organized a search of Agar and Fanny's old lodgings at 3 Cambridge Villas. This occurred on 22 September and the house was uninhabited at the time. Everything he saw confirmed the facts of Fanny's story. He went up to the back room on the first floor where there was a stove in the fireplace. Rees had the stove removed and, sure enough, behind it he found the fire-bricks. He noticed that the chimney was 'entirely free from soot, and had evidently been subjected to a very intense heat'. The bricks also had 'appearances of gold on them'. He noticed that the floor-boards were 'burnt in several places, principally in front of the fire place, between the fire place and the window'. He had these boards taken up 'where the burning was' and found 'several small particles of gold' underneath: 'They had evidently dropped through the boards onto the ceiling below.'[12]

Then Rees got permission from the Secretary of State to interview Agar at Portland Prison, where he was being held pending his transportation to Australia. At first Rees did not say anything to Agar about what he had discovered at Cambridge Villas and Agar did not even know that he had been there. On this first visit, which took place around the first week of October 1856, the prisoner 'made no communication' with him. It was only on Rees's second visit, ten days or a fortnight later, that Agar began to tell his story for the first time. By then Agar had found out about Pierce's treachery and was particularly angered by the effect that Pierce's behaviour would have on his son's future welfare: '... I had heard that Pierce had sent it [i.e. the child] to its mother – Pierce had the charge of it when I was arrested – I had heard that the mother was in a state of distress, and he had sent the child, but would not give it a change of clothing.'[13]

Because of what Agar now told them, the police went on the trail of William Pierce. It is no surprise, seeing how he had benefitted from the train robbery, that he was doing nicely for himself; he had part ownership of a lucrative betting-shop in Panton Street, Haymarket, and he kept a private account at the London & Commercial Bank.[14] All of this was brought crashing down, however, on 5 November 1856, when he was arrested and his house at Kilburn Villa was searched. Led by Agar's statement, Rees went down into the cellar and found a sort of pantry running underneath the front steps. He noticed that the ground had been disturbed in one place where a hole had obviously been dug. There was, however, no gold present. The hole had been filled in with loose cinders, leaves, berries and rubbish. Rees determined that it had been filled in quite recently from the freshness of the leaves and the autumn berries and the condition of part of the claw of a lobster that was also in there. This, he concluded, was the hole in which Pierce had, until recently, hidden the gold from the train robbery.

Inspector Frederick Williamson and Sergeant Smith accompanied Rees to the house in Kilburn Villa. They discovered several boxes there, including a green tool-box in the attic, with two pieces of leather and some tools inside. A number of items were removed from the house as evidence: Turkish bonds amounting to about £2,600, memorandums, deeds, leases, securities for money, IOUs, promissory notes and at least one betting book. There was also a gold watch with a representation of Windsor Castle on the face and the initials 'E.R.A.' on the back – Agar's initials – along with a chain.

The authorities had now reached the point where they had to move against the other suspects. On the same day as Pierce was arrested, Burgess was taken from his train by the police. Tester was still out of the country, in Sweden, and so could not be arrested, but the authorities made it clear that they wanted him to return to England in order to face the charges against him.

Arrests may have finally been made in the case of the Great Train Robbery, but no one could be sure whether the evidence against the men arrested would be strong enough to lead even to a trial, never mind successful convictions.

CHAPTER 12

Mansion House

Fanny and Agar had come forward with their stories, but the next step was to determine whether Pierce, Burgess and Tester, if he could be apprehended, really had a legal case to answer. Consequently, on 6 November 1856, the day after their arrests, Pierce and Burgess were brought before a hearing at the Mansion House in London, to determine whether they should stand trial for the crime of 'having stolen £15,000 worth of bullion from a package in a carriage of the South Eastern Railway'.[1] They arrived in the custody of Sergeant Smith. The hearing was presided over by the Lord Mayor, in his capacity as Chief Magistrate of the city.

Word had spread that the train robbers had been apprehended and a crowd gathered outside the Mansion House to witness the spectacle. Once the proceedings had commenced, Mr Bodkin, on behalf of the prosecution, informed the Lord Mayor about the importance of their main witness who, as yet, remained unnamed:

He has told the whole story of this robbery with such deliberation and minuteness that we have been able to trace out matters that confirm his statement in almost every important particular, and certainly it will be my duty to lay before your Lordship evidence which will at all events make it imperative upon you to remand them to a future day in order that we may bring home to them the enormous offence with which they are charged.[2]

Agar may have been unnamed in court, but his identity was quite widely known. Rees assured the Lord Mayor about the guilt of the prisoners standing before him: 'They were taken into custody yesterday by my authority, and I believe, if a remand takes place, I shall be in a condition to produce evidence affecting them both, touching the present charge. I have no doubt to be able to show their guilty participation in the robbery.'[3] Yet, as Rees explained, the prosecution needed more time in order to produce their star witness from Portland Prison. They would have to '... make an application to the Secretary of State or the proper authority to secure his attendance here'.[4]

Burgess complained to the Lord Mayor that he lacked legal representation. With an amazing degree of audacity in the circumstances, he stated that he felt he had been let down by his employers, the South Eastern Railway Company: 'I have not been treated very fairly by this company,' he said, 'who have not taken my cause in hand.'[5] He had, he told the court, attempted to engage a Mr Humphries as his counsel, and had even met with the gentleman that very morning, but Humphries refused to take the case and he was now left without representation. Wontner, who was appearing for Pierce, told the court that Burgess had asked him if he would 'watch the case for him' as well, but Wontner was reluctant to do so: 'I told the man that I did not feel that I ought to do so, not being concerned for him, and not knowing whether the interests of the men might clash at all.'[6] In Bodkin's opinion there was no difficulty in Wontner representing both of the prisoners: 'What you will say and do for the one you will say and do for the other.' The Lord Mayor had no sympathy for Burgess's plight either:

> From my long experience it is my duty to say that there is nothing whatever at present affecting either of you. Pierce is advised and defended; you are not. There is nothing at present in this case, except the opinion of a professional man, who has seen a witness who it is supposed will affect your character.

The case has been opened, and probably before you appear here again some professional man will attend and protect you.[7]

The next comment from the Lord Mayor made his lack of sympathy abundantly clear: 'As far as I myself am concerned, I am sorry to see a railway guard of many years' standing – one of a most respectable class of our population – standing at the bar upon a charge of this kind.'[8] As there was no witness present in court and no evidence being produced, apart from the assertion being made by the prosecution side that such would soon be forthcoming, Wontner appealed for both prisoners to be set free immediately:

> This is a case in which I submit there is no evidence whatever. We have simply the opinion and belief of a gentleman. But the law does not allow magistrates or judges or anybody else to act upon opinions and belief which are not based upon legitimate evidence. There is no evidence before your lordship to justify these people being remanded, except the belief of this gentleman that he will be able at a future period to produce evidence against them.[9]
>
> There is nothing whatever to implicate these parties in the transaction, and, sitting here as a magistrate bound to receive and to decide upon legal evidence before you ... I think you will feel that you are not justified in detaining the parties.[10]

Pierce and Burgess were not, according to Wontner, the kind of defendants who were likely to flee:

> The witness for years past has known Pierce's address. Burgess, I understand, is a railway guard in the employment of the company even up to the present hour. He was taken off the train last night. The company, therefore, are not dealing with persons likely to fly from an investigation, and it is monstrous to ask you to detain these men because the solicitor to the company chooses to come into the box and to state his belief

that upon some future occasion he will be able to make out a case against them.[11]

The Lord Mayor, however, did not go along with this thinking, and declared himself satisfied with the assurances given that a witness would be produced to 'substantiate the case'.[12] He therefore remanded the prisoners in custody.

At least one group of interested spectators knew who the witness was and were disappointed that he had not shown up in court; a number of bankers had arrived just to have a look at their old adversary, Agar the forger and fraudster. Their presence was noted by the press: 'During the past week several of the metropolitan bankers have applied for admission, in order that they might see Agar, whom they suspect to be the author of the various forgeries from which they have suffered during recent years, and the perpetrators of which they have never yet been able to discover.'[13] As a result of Agar's non-appearance the bankers were, instead, 'referred to the Secretary of State for permission to see the convict in Millbank Penitentiary', where he was to be detained during the hearing.[14]

A few days later, on 12 November 1856, the hearing assembled at the Mansion House once again. On 10 November, between the first and second hearings, a new Lord Mayor, Thomas Quested Finnis, had been inaugurated and he now took over the proceedings. The prisoners arrived in the custody of Sergeant Smith and Inspector Thornton.[15] Bodkin, instructed by Rees, represented the South Eastern Railway Company, while Pierce was again represented by Wontner. This time Burgess had his own legal counsel in the person of a Mr Lewis. Tester, still working in Sweden, was not present, although there were rumours that he was about to return to England in order to surrender himself voluntarily and, it was said, to vindicate his reputation. Bodkin introduced the case to the new Lord Mayor:

Your Lordship is no doubt aware that these two prisoners are charged by the South Eastern Railway Company with having, in the year 1855, been concerned in the stealing of a large quantity of gold ... which was being conveyed by that railway from this country to France. Your Lordship's predecessor heard Mr Rees ... state upon his oath that he believed he should be in a condition, and indeed, knew that he should be in a position, to produce material evidence bringing this charge home to both the prisoners if they were remanded until to-day. Your Lordship's predecessor, upon that statement, was pleased to remand them accordingly.[16]

But it soon became evident that, once again, there was a problem with the appearance of the secret witness. Agar was not present. Bodkin was keen to stress that this was not down to any negligence on the part of the prosecution: '... those who bring a charge against any of their fellow subjects are bound to use every possible diligence in bringing forward evidence to support it; and there has been no lack of industry on the part of those who prosecute this case....'[17] Once again, however, they had failed to produce their witness: 'I regret to state that, without any fault or want of diligence on our part, but entirely through the necessity of going through certain forms in order to procure the attendance of that witness, who is a convict under sentence ... at Portland, we are not in a position to produce him to-day.'[18] They were, however, according to Bodkin, not far away from achieving their goal, and he implored the Lord Mayor to have patience and give them a little more time: 'He cannot arrive in London till late this afternoon, but then we are certain that he will be here; and, therefore, at any hour that your Lordship will appoint this case to go on tomorrow we shall be in a condition to carry out our intention by commencing the case with his examination.'[19] The Lord Mayor sought some further reassurances from Bodkin that they had not been tardy about requesting the necessary permissions needed to present their witness in court. Bodkin assured his Lordship that they had done everything possible and, in fact, 'instantly after the remand a communication was made to the Home-office....'[20]

While all this was going on the prisoners were still in custody. Understandably, Wontner objected on Pierce's behalf. He once again requested that his client be released immediately. He complained that the previous Lord Mayor had been wrong in remanding the prisoners 'without the slightest evidence having been adduced against them'.[21] He also aired a fresh grievance; he complained about the behaviour of the South Eastern Railway towards Pierce. He claimed that representatives of that company had been paying visits to Pierce's home 'three or four times a day' and had been offensive to Pierce's family. He urged, accordingly, that his client be released.

Lewis, when he spoke on behalf of Burgess, concurred with the opinion that the prisoners should be released. He said that the solicitor for the prosecution simply saying that he had been told something by someone else would not be taken as evidence in any court. The South Eastern Railway Company had had ample opportunity to bring charges against Burgess, he said, if there had been any cause to do so. In fact, the evidence was to the contrary, for months after the robbery his client was still a loyal employee of that company. Moreover, Lewis argued that the crime had actually taken place outside the jurisdiction of the Lord Mayor's court.

In the end, though, neither the pleadings of Wontner nor Lewis held any sway with the new Lord Mayor. He was not prepared to release the prisoners – at least not yet: 'My predecessor, upon the former occasion, remanded these parties, after hearing the evidence which was then given, and therefore I consider that I am bound upon the same evidence to remand them until tomorrow.'[22] But it was clear that time was running out for the prosecution. Although the Lord Mayor had expressed confidence that the witness would appear in court at their next sitting, the fact that he explicitly stated that he would remand the prisoners 'until tomorrow' must have sounded ominous to the prosecution. All in all, it had been a very inauspicious start to the proceedings. The whole case seemed to be on very shaky ground and it could collapse. The prospects for the prisoners were growing more and more encouraging. Many wondered what lay behind this delay in getting Agar to court. When it came to it, would a lifelong criminal like Agar really turn informer? Surely this was the great unwritten taboo of the criminal world, of which Agar had been a member all his life. As angry as he was with Pierce, and as concerned for the welfare of Fanny and his son as he was, would he be willing to inform on his accomplices? It all seemed to be hanging by a thread, and the following day would be crucial. If the prosecution failed to get Agar to court and ready to testify, Pierce and Burgess would surely be granted their freedom.

CHAPTER 13

One of a Class Too Numerous

———•———

The hearing before the Lord Mayor at the Mansion House convened for the third time on 13 November 1856. Pierce and Burgess must have felt somewhat dejected when the rumour circulated around the court that Agar was finally present. Bodkin announced the arrival of his main witness with no small hint of triumphalism: 'My Lord Mayor, in accordance with the understanding that we came to yesterday, we are now in a condition to proceed with this very extraordinary and important inquiry. The witness who was adverted to yesterday has arrived, and is in attendance and will be examined.'[1] Those who thought that Agar would never give evidence against his criminal accomplices were about to be proved wrong. Bodkin proceeded to outline the main details of the case for the benefit of the Lord Mayor and the large crowd in attendance. He emphasized the daring and unique nature of the crime committed: '... this robbery was committed with great deliberation, great adroitness, and ... four persons, so far as our evidence now extends, were concerned in its commission....'[2] He was finally able to reveal the name of his witness: '... the man whom I may now name Edward Agar ... will be a witness on the part of the Crown.' He also informed the Lord Mayor that another suspect in this crime, William Tester, had not yet been apprehended as he was not in the country. Bodkin admitted that his witness, Agar, was 'not unfamiliar with crime, and probably was one of a class too numerous in this great metropolis, who are engaged systematically in the commission of what are called large offences'. But, he stated, Agar was willing to give evidence because of the way in which his former criminal associate, Pierce, had treated his child and its mother.[3] Pierce had, Bodkin informed the hearing, deprived the woman and child of the financial means that Agar had provided for them. 'That woman and child,' he said, 'were turned adrift by Pierce.'[4] He tried to emphasize the notion that Agar's reason for giving evidence was a laudable one: ' ... the natural affection that he had for that woman and that child, proving, as it is indeed indisputable by every day's experience, that "one touch of nature makes the whole world kin." That I think will appear to have been his motive.'[5] He concluded his opening statement by urging the Lord Mayor to send the prisoners for trial: '... I have no doubt your Lordship will feel it your duty to send this case for trial, and that a jury will be constrained to find them guilty of the offence with which they are charged.'[6]

One can only wonder at the great sense of anticipation in the courtroom as the time came for Agar to take the stand. He began, in response to prosecution questions, by admitting openly his involvement in the robbery. He then explained that it had been Pierce's idea from the beginning. He told of their various trips to Folkestone in preparation for the job and their careful observations of the activities there. He outlined the details of how they had actually carried out the crime. Agar had not finished his testimony when the hearing was adjourned until the following Monday, 17 November 1856.

On that day, Agar was brought to court under the supervision of Captain Craig, the deputy governor of Millbank Prison.[7] As news of the proceedings spread, the interest from the public was growing ever greater and crowds of people were trying to gain entry to the Mansion House: '... a body of police were placed at the gates of the Mansion House to preserve order and keep back several hundred people who had congregated long before the court opened, and who remained in the street the whole of the day in the vain expectation of gaining admission.'[8] The examination of the witness continued and Agar told the hearing how he and Pierce had disposed of some of the proceeds of the train robbery. He explained how they had melted down the gold. One of the fire-bricks that Pierce had bought to put around the very hot fire was produced in court. Agar examined it and identified it as such. Some pieces of gold were still stuck to it.[9]

In the course of his evidence Agar mentioned the name of the barrister, James Townsend Saward. This was the first time that Saward's involvement with criminality had been exposed publicly. Agar explained how he had sold some of the stolen gold to Saward. We can only wonder whether this revelation about one of their colleagues caused any embarrassment among those members of the legal profession present. In response to questions from Bodkin and Lewis, Agar said that Saward 'called himself a barrister' and was also 'a pigeon fancier'. To this, Lewis replied: 'And a gold fancier', which caused laughter in court.[10] These revelations about Saward did not come as a surprise to those on the prosecution side, however, as Agar had, it seems, told them all about his criminal associate and his illegal practices. A whole world of crime in London and elsewhere was being revealed and this would have serious repercussions for Saward and his gang.

Agar explained that when he was arrested a substantial amount of the haul from the train robbery still remained to be sold. He explained that Pierce had been left in full possession of this after he was arrested and convicted. Agar told the hearing about the financial arrangements that he tried to put in place for the benefit of Fanny and his child, and how Pierce had betrayed him, leaving the woman and child destitute.

When they got their opportunity to cross-examine Agar, the defence strategy was to reveal him as a professional crook. He did, however, defend himself stoutly in the various exchanges with counsel. He resolutely refused to be called a forger:[11]

Lewis: You have admitted yourself to be convicted of forgery, to be a thief, to have forged false keys, and to be a conspirator....

Agar: I am not a forger. I never was a forger.

Lewis: When did you first commence uttering forged instruments?

Agar: I never uttered any forged instruments. I was convicted of forgery, but it was through a mistake on the part of a man who swore falsely. I never uttered a forged instrument in my life.

He wanted to draw a rather dubious distinction between being a forger and making money from forgery:

Lewis: Within ten or a dozen years ... how many times have you received the proceeds of forgery?

Agar: Probably four or five.

Lewis: Were they large amounts that you received as the result of the forgeries?

Agar: No; small amounts.

The name of his old accomplice, William Nash, who had been transported for his forgery activities with Agar some years previously, was then raised:

Lewis: Do you know a man named Nash who was transported?

Agar: Yes.

Lewis: Did you and he have anything to do with forged cheques?

Agar: That has nothing to do with this case ... I have told you that I have been connected with several forgeries, but I do not think this person named Nash has anything to do with the case.

Lewis: Was Nash a friend of yours?

Agar: He was an acquaintance of mine.

Lewis: Did you ever receive from him the proceeds of any forged cheques or bills?

Agar: Never. I have received money from him for various things.

Lewis: Have those various things been the result of forgeries
   or robberies?
Agar: I do not think I am bound to answer these questions. It
   has nothing to do with the case.

This line of questioning came to an end when the Lord Mayor
intervened and told Agar: 'It has nothing to do with the case ...
you are not bound to answer these questions unless you feel
inclined to do so.' He did not feel inclined to do so. He was then
asked about his many aliases:

Lewis: In the last 12 years how many names have you
   assumed?
Agar: Adams, Agar, Whitfield, Richardson, and Archer.
   Adams is the principal name ... but my real name is Agar.

He told the court that Samuel Seal, who had been arrested for
being involved in the robbery, had nothing at all to do with it.
He laughed when he was asked why he did not think it necessary
to come forward at the time of Mr Seal's arrest: '... I did not care
about it ...' he said simply and rather callously.[12] He then gave
details, under cross-examination, about his trips in Burgess's
van, which must have been of great interest to the representatives of the South Eastern Railway present: 'As soon as the key
was made we took every opportunity of trying it. It was always
in his van ... At times there would be a carriage between us and
the engineman and stoker. There is a window on the top of the
van from which the guard could see the engine-driver. The guard
can see the engineman and stoker from his van....' But, he
replied in answer to a query from Bodkin, they were working in
a section of the van from which they could not be seen. The
reason for all these detailed questions was to demonstrate that
Agar had an intimate knowledge of Burgess's working environment. This was important because whether Pierce and Burgess
would stand trial for this crime depended on the degree to which
the Lord Mayor found Agar a credible witness. Was he telling

the truth or was he a villain simply trying to incriminate innocent people? The level of detail in a story could indicate whether
a witness was telling the truth or not. Of course, although Agar's
evidence was crucial, so too would be the corroboration of his
story by other witnesses.

When Agar had concluded giving his evidence, Fanny Kay
was the next witness called. As news of this sensational case had
spread both through the newspapers and word of mouth, there
was huge interest in getting a look at this woman who had first
exposed the details of the train robbery. She was described by
the press, for a reading public hungry for details, as having 'a
very intelligent countenance' and being 'a respectable looking
young woman'.[13] Obviously relations between her and Agar
were still very good and she was not shy about showing it: '...
the moment she entered she shook hands with great apparent
cordiality with Agar.'[14] She spoke honestly and openly about
their relationship and the child they had together. The boy, she
told them, was two years old on the previous 7 July.[15] She
explained how she knew Pierce and Burgess and how they were
'upon intimate terms' with Agar.[16] To underline this she gave
details of Pierce's frequent visits to their house at Cambridge
Villas. 'We breakfasted about 7 o'clock,' she said, 'and he generally came to breakfast, and used to remain till 5 o'clock and take
his meals with us.'[17] And of the secret activities he and her
husband were involved in there she said: 'They frequently used
the washhouse. They were in the washhouse sometimes from
breakfast to dinner time. I could not see what they were doing.
The windows were whitened, and the doors fastened. They used
to be hammering very much sometimes, and I have heard them
filing....'[18] She was also able to testify to the fact that both Pierce
and Agar knew Tester: 'I know a person named Tester. I have
seen him at Tunbridge [Wells]. I have heard Pierce and Agar
speak of Tester.'[19] She explained what happened between her
and Pierce following Agar's arrest and conviction. She had lived
with Mr and Mrs Pierce for a while, she said, but that did not
work out and she explained the dire financial circumstances in

The shot tower where the gang bought the lead shot that would later be
used to replace the weight of the stolen gold and other valuables

The busy Tooley Street in London where the gang members met to plan
the first great train robbery

The robbers stole the gold from the wooden boxes in which it was being transported and replaced it with lead shot in order to keep the weight constant. This picture shows one of these boxes, still containing the lead shot, held today by the National Railway Museum

London Bridge Station, the location for the South Eastern Railway's terminus and the place where the robbers boarded the train that night

Until that night in May 1855 the South Eastern Railway Company had handled numerous shipments of gold and other valuables from London to Paris every week without incident

Folkestone Pier: the departure point for the quickest available route to continental Europe

AGAR, THE APPROVER.

Edward Agar was a career criminal, described as 'small and thin with an oval-shaped face, light brown hair and grey eyes'

TESTER, THE RAILWAY CLERK.

William George Tester, the twenty-five-year-old railway clerk with a sallow complexion, an impressive moustache and whiskers, dark hazel eyes and a liking for 'fashionable attire'

James Burgess had been a long-time, loyal employee of the South Eastern Railway Company like his father before him

An artist's impression of the arrest of James Townsend Saward, also known as Jim the Penman, the infamous barrister, crook and associate of Edward Agar

BURGESS, THE GUARD.

"HE WAS FOUND AT LAST IN A COFFEE-SHOP"

which Pierce had since left her, in strict contravention of Agar's wishes. The story she told of how Pierce had treated a vulnerable woman and child did not endear him to anyone: 'After I left Pierce's house I wrote to him, being very ill, asking him to send me £10, which he did. That was the last money I received from him. I think that was last May ... His wife has given me 10s. sometimes.'[20] Pierce treated her and her son badly even though, she said, he was not short of money: 'I have seen, while at Pierce's, a great quantity of banknotes.'[21] To make matters worse, a lot of that money was Agar's. She told of a time when she had gone back to Pierce's house to pick up some of the child's clothes and how, according to her, he had abused her physically: 'I waited some time to see Pierce. I should think it was about half-past 9 o'clock when he came home. I was sitting in the kitchen, and he came down and asked me what I wanted to see him for. I told him I wanted my child's clothes, and he said, "Do you?" and he dragged me down upon the floor by the hair of my head.'[22]

As Fanny concluded her evidence, the Lord Mayor decided that it was a convenient time to bring the proceedings of the day to a close. Before that could be done, however, Lewis once again called for Burgess to be granted bail: '... the only evidence,' he said, 'which at all affected him was that of Agar, whose testimony was not to be relied upon.'[23] Once again the Lord Mayor disagreed and refused the request.

With the conclusion of the evidence given by Agar and Fanny, the major part of the case against the prisoners had been presented to the Lord Mayor. What followed would mostly be important as corroboration of their testimony. Would the witnesses to come have seen and heard enough to verify what had already been stated? The prisoners were remanded until the following Monday.

CHAPTER 14

The Promise of Return

When the hearing at the Mansion House sat again at 10.30 a.m. on Monday, 24 November 1856, the prisoners came under the careful scrutiny of the press as they entered: 'They were both as cool and collected in their demeanour as on the previous occasions, though they looked somewhat paler. Burgess still retains his dress as a guard of the South Eastern Railway.'[1] The newspapers pondered the events of the previous day and imagined what the prisoners must have made of it: '... both prisoners evidently appeared surprised, after what was said at the last examination, that Seward [sic] and Tester were not placed in the dock beside them.'[2]

Charlotte Paynter began the day's proceedings by giving evidence of her time working for Agar and Fanny as a servant at both Harleyford Road, Vauxhall, and Cambridge Villas, Shepherd's Bush. She said that Pierce, whom she only ever knew as Peckham, was a frequent visitor to their home. Like Fanny, she told of Pierce and Agar's strange activities in the wash-house at Cambridge Villas and described a number of suspiciously heavy boxes around the house and a leather bag that she had seen there.[3] Under cross-examination, Charlotte admitted to the fact that Rees had paid her two shillings for agreeing to be examined on what she had seen and a further two shillings when he took her to Mrs Porter's, Agar's landlady, and asked her further questions in Mrs Porter's presence. She also admitted that the material she had read in the papers about this case had 'refreshed' her memory.[4] These facts, the defence hoped, might cast doubt on the veracity of her evidence.

The testimony of Mary Ann Wilde, the domestic servant from next door, did not progress matters greatly. She merely told of 'sometimes' seeing Agar going into his wash-house with another man who, she said, she could neither remember nor identify.[5] She did remember the sound of hammering coming from the property.

Mary Ann Porter, Agar's landlady, was able to verify the close relationship that existed between Agar and Pierce. She explained that Agar, whom she knew as Mr Adams, took lodgings from her for himself and Mrs Adams for about seven weeks in the period before Christmas 1854. She noticed that Pierce, or as he was known to her, Mr Peckham, was a frequent visitor there who sometimes stayed 'half the day, and sometimes longer'.[6] The couple moved out, she said, about a week before Christmas and Mr Peckham helped them to move.

Two cab drivers, Mr Ellis and Joseph Carter, were called on to give evidence regarding the movements of two men around the time of the train robbery. Ellis gave descriptions that appeared very similar to Pierce and Agar, while Carter was actually able to identify Pierce and Agar in court. They both told of driving the men to and from St Thomas Street, and of their suspicious activities with bags of various sizes.[7] When he was asked if he had ever been in court before, Carter caused merriment when he declared that he had been, but only once, for 'intoxication – and he got off'.[8]

Mr Clements, the former owner of a coffee-shop 'by the turnpike adjoining the Southampton Arms', said that he remembered seeing the same two men, with bags, at his business on one occasion around the same time. John Honnor, a hairdresser and Pierce's neighbour in Lambeth Walk near Walnut Tree Walk, stated that he had dressed a wig for Pierce. Pierce had told him that it was 'for a friend of his, an elderly gentleman'.[9] John Allday, a schoolboy, told of how he and his friends found a quantity of lead shot dumped around the area of Prince's Terrace, not far from Crown Terrace.

Walter Stearn, proprietor of the White Hart public house in St Thomas Street, was able to identify Pierce and Burgess. His premises were a favourite haunt of railway staff, being only two or three minutes away from London Bridge station, and Pierce and Burgess were both frequent customers of his.[10] Stearn also testified to the fact that in the period after the train robbery, the previous February, 1856, Burgess was in possession of a considerable amount of money because Stearn had deposited £500 for him with his brewers, Messrs Reids.[11] Burgess had told him that the money represented 'the saving of years'.[12] Sarah Thompson, the barmaid, was able to concur with this evidence, as she had given Burgess his interest of £8 1s 1d, along with showing him the account book.

As if the testimony of the witnesses was not entertaining enough for the public, there was an extra sideshow when a man present in court, Robert Dackombe, was accused of communicating with Pierce. James Porter, a carpenter from Harleyford Road and the husband of Mary Ann Porter who gave evidence earlier, claimed that he saw a man speak to Pierce in a whisper on the previous day, and asserted that Dackombe was that man. 'I am sure he is the person,' Porter declared confidently to the Lord Mayor.[13] Although he said that he could not actually hear what Dackombe had said, Porter did claim to have heard Pierce's answer, which cannot have been very comforting for the witnesses present, as it was: 'Make away with them – destroy them.'[14] Dackombe was then called on to answer the accusation. He was described as 'a stout, big man, with a ruddy complexion' who said he was 'a coach proprietor ... a liveryman and a freeman of the Pewterers' Company'.[15] Dackombe declared himself to be totally innocent of the accusation: 'I ... never have had the least charge brought against me upon any one occasion; and as to speaking to Pierce I did not go near him ... I never spoke to him in the court the whole time.'[16] He did admit that he knew Pierce. He even once bought a horse from him, but that was, he said, 'in the presence of a respectable coach proprietor'.[17] Despite Dackombe's protestations of innocence, Porter's accusations were supported by Inspector Mitchell of the City of London police. With reference to Dackombe, Mitchell said: 'At the close of the examination last Monday I saw this person ... I do not know his name, speak to Pierce from the back of the dock. I leant forward, to endeavour to catch what was said, but did not succeed.'[18] Bodkin asked him if he was sure that Dackombe was the person in question, to which he replied: 'I am sure....'[19] The Lord Mayor then asked the inspector why, therefore, in his professional capacity, had he not interfered to prevent the conversation taking place? Mitchell replied: 'I had no charge of the prisoners; they were in charge of other officers. Still, I consider it a portion of my duty to try and hear anything that was said, although I was unable to do so. Very few words passed.'[20] The Lord Mayor was, in the end, unconvinced that anything significant had passed between Dackombe and Pierce, but he did impress on those whose responsibility it was to prevent such an occurrence from taking place that they should take every precaution in the future 'to prevent prisoners whilst in the dock having communication with bystanders in the court'.[21] No more action was taken on the matter, and the hearing was adjourned until the following week.

There was yet more drama when the hearing reconvened on 2 December 1856 and Mr Bodkin announced that it was his understanding that Tester would be presenting himself before the Lord Mayor on the next day that they sat. He had, it was announced, decided to return to England and face the charges against him. There was some discussion whether, in that event, the proceedings should continue at all for that day. In the end it was decided to continue hearing witnesses whose evidence it would not be necessary to repeat for Tester, in the event of his turning up. Therefore, Charles Bessell, Agar and Fanny's neighbour at Cambridge Villas, was called. His function was merely to verify that Agar and Fanny were his neighbours there. Next came Zaccheus Long, who stated that he rented his house at 4 Crown Terrace to Pierce from 18 December 1854 to 18 June 1855.[22] He had no complaints at all to make about his former tenant: 'I received my rent of him, and judged that he was in prosperous circumstances. I supposed he was well to do in the world ... he settled everything before he left.'[23] John Carter said that Pierce moved to his house at 3 Crown Terrace in June 1855. He was able to identify him even though his hair was, he said, 'much shorter' then.[24]

It was determined that anything Rees might have to say in his testimony would have no bearing on Tester's innocence or guilt, so he too was called to give evidence. Rees told the Lord Mayor about searching Pierce's house and finding evidence of the hole in which, he believed, some of the stolen gold had been hidden. He also said that he had interviewed Burgess many months before, not long after he came to the job, but the man refused to admit to anything.[25] He denied, in response to Lewis's cross-examination, that he had told Burgess he would 'intercede with the Secretary of State for the purpose of getting him a pardon' if he told him all about the robbery: 'I did not tell him that if he made a disclosure he should go free. I said nothing at all to that effect.'[26] Lewis pushed the matter further:

> Lewis: Do you remember saying to the prisoner Burgess, 'I have no authority from the directors to promise you anything; but I have no doubt if you will give your evidence correctly that we can save you?'
> Rees: No.
> Lewis: Nothing to that effect?
> Rees: No.
> Lewis: Are you on your oath?
> Rees: I am.
> Lewis: What is your answer?
> Rees: I did not say so.
> Lewis: Burgess says the conversation took place while Hall was present.
> Rees: It did.
> Lewis: Does that bring it to your mind?
> Rees: No; I have no doubt that I gave him some advice as to

the expediency of telling me everything he knew. I gave him advice. I told him that on an occasion of this sort it was better to state all he knew. I certainly held out no inducement to him.

Bodkin then asked Rees, 'Whatever passed between you, he persisted in denying all knowledge of the robbery?', and Rees answered, 'Most distinctly.'

The day was brought to a close with the evidence of Emma May, who worked at the Marquis of Granby public house. She was able to testify to the fact that Burgess and Pierce were often in the pub together along with another man who she described as 'tall' with 'a full face' and 'rather dark':[27]

> May: He [Burgess] used to say to me, 'Emma, are my friends come?'
> Bodkin: Did you then see who he meant by his friends when he asked for them – whom did he join?
> May: Pierce and another.

The hearing was then adjourned for a week. All interest was now focused upon the question of whether William Tester would really appear before the Lord Mayor at the next sitting.

CHAPTER 15

A Voluntary Surrender

———•———

In the aftermath of the announcement that Tester planned to surrender himself to the Lord Mayor at the Mansion House there was much speculation in the press regarding this remarkable development. The prosecution and the police were reported to be far from magnanimous regarding Tester's planned surrender and, it was reported, were doing their best to capture him before the next sitting at the Mansion House. Their aim was, according to the press, '… by his capture to deprive him of any merit or appearance of innocence which might attach to a voluntary surrender'.[1] Those representing Tester, for their part, began preparing the way for his appearance by leaking his version of events to the press: '… it is understood that he gives a general and complete denial to the charge made against him, and affirms that he neither took part in the deliberations which preceded the robbery, nor shared even to the smallest extent in the proceeds of the robbery after its accomplishment.'[2] Tester did admit to being 'well acquainted with Burgess' and having 'some knowledge of Pierce' through his work with the railway. He also admitted 'that Agar was not unknown to him' as 'a frequent traveller on the line' but 'there was no sort of intimacy between them'.[3] He had always believed, he said, that Agar was a 'commercial traveller'.[4] Anyway, he argued that any evidence coming from a man like Agar was worthless: '… it is, perhaps, not too much to say that the uncorroborated evidence of Agar could convict no man, even upon a charge of small importance.'[5]

Tester must have believed this. He was of the opinion that Agar's reputation was such that his evidence would fail to convict or even send the defendants to trial. This, evidently, prompted his decision to return to England. His friends at any rate were advising him thus. It was, however, contrary to the advice of his more experienced legal representatives. Those with prior knowledge of such matters knew that returning to England was a very risky strategy.

Then, in yet another twist, it was reported that Tester had been dismissed from his position with the Swedish Railways some weeks earlier. According to Tester himself, he had been 'suddenly dismissed' from his position 'without any cause being assigned by the authorities'. Now he suspected that this had happened because someone had informed them of Agar's accusations about him. He said that after his dismissal he had decided to return to England, travelling via Copenhagen, Hamburg, Belgium and Calais, and it was only on the journey home that he learned of Agar's statement and concluded that that was the reason for his dismissal.[6]

Despite the desire on the part of the police to capture him, Tester had arrived in Dover and stood on the platform at the railway station there for nearly an hour, unnoticed, with his only disguise being an upturned coat collar. He also passed through his old place of employment, London Bridge station, without anyone from the South Eastern Railway Company recognizing him: '... without inquiry, or even a suspicion being entertained that the man upon whom the company were, above all others, anxious to lay their hands had so easily eluded pursuit.'[7]

Ironically, Rees travelled down the very same railway line to Dover that night in order to meet Tester's father and inquire about his son's whereabouts.[8]

Understandably, with the news that Tester was about to appear, there was even more interest in the proceedings at the Mansion House. At the next sitting, on 10 December, a Mr Buchanan addressed the Lord Mayor and declared that he was Tester's solicitor. He said that his client had now returned to

England and was ready to present himself before the Lord Mayor. Buchanan announced that Tester was, in fact, only five minutes away and would surrender himself to the hearing if he could be assured that he would not be arrested on the way: '... I expect that faith will be observed, and that he will not be pounced upon by an officer in the street, but that he may come and surrender.'[9]

This was agreed and in actuality it took Tester ten minutes to arrive. He walked in wearing what was described as 'fashionable attire' and was led to the dock to join Pierce and Burgess. He looked pale and anxious.[10] He was asked for his Christian name, to which he replied, in a firm voice, 'William George'.[11] The evidence that had been heard up to that point in the proceedings was then read out for the benefit of Tester and his legal counsel. Once this had been done, the next portion of the hearing was taken up with the testimonies of a number of bank employees, clerks and stockbrokers, who all gave information regarding various alleged illegal financial transactions that had been carried out in exchange for the haul stolen from the train.

Agar was then recalled to the witness-box and asked to identify Mr Tester formally, which he did by referring to him as the man 'on the left side of Burgess'.[12] A number of witnesses from Folkestone followed. Harriet Hooker, the proprietor, with her husband, of the lodging-house in which Agar and Pierce had stayed on one of their visits to Folkestone, gave details of the men's time there. In order for her to attempt an identification of him, Agar was led into the room once again and asked to stand amid a group of people; Mrs Hooker had no difficulty in pointing him out. Charles Chapman, the clerk at Folkestone for the South Eastern Railway, told of his encounters with Agar in 1854. Superintendant Steer of the Folkestone police detailed his various observations and suspicions of Agar, Pierce and Burgess. When Thomas Sharman, the other clerk from Folkestone, was called on to testify and give his account of sharing sherry and biscuits with Agar and Tester in the Pavilion Hotel, the defence put it to him that he had associated with Agar just as closely as the defendants in the dock had:

> Lewis: ... he was your companion that you drank with?
>
> Sharman: Oh, no.
>
> Lewis: If you are going to say that he was a companion of those men [Burgess and Tester], let us see whether he was a companion of yours.
>
> Sharman: He was not of mine. I did not go to the cigar shop to smoke with them, nor to the hotel to dine. I did to drink. I did not walk out with him ... afterwards....
>
> Lewis: You were in company with this convict and forger as well as the others?
>
> Sharman: He was not a convict then.
>
> Lewis: He deserved to be a convict, according to his own account. He was not a convict when these men [Burgess and Tester] walked with him. You did what these men did – walked with him?
>
> Sharman: On that occasion.
>
> Lewis: And if you stood there [pointing to the dock] evidence might have been given that you drank with them, and were seen in their company. That is precisely the same thing.
>
> Sharman: No doubt it is; precisely the same.[13]

With that, Lewis had finished making a point that had far more to do with his own client's case than Sharman's evidence. The hearing then adjourned.

When the proceedings reconvened on Saturday, 13 December 1856, the interest among the public was still, as *The Times* put it, 'intense'.[14] The first witness called to give evidence was Inspector Hazel of the South Eastern Railway Police. Hazel testified about the number of times that he had seen Agar, Pierce and Tester at Folkestone in 1854, and the suspicious nature of their activities there. When he saw Agar and Tester together, he said, they seemed '... to be on very friendly terms with each other'.[15] Mr Werter Clark, the owner of the Rose Inn in Dover, and

Robert Clark, the waiter at the Dover Castle Hotel, told of the two mysterious men who had frequented their respective establishments.[16] Henry Williams and Joseph Witherden, the booking clerk and porter at Dover Station, were called and were asked about the two strangers who had passed through their station on the night of the robbery itself.[17] Matthew Dickenson and William Woodhouse from London Bridge station also gave evidence regarding the arrival of the same two men in London that night.

Stephen Jones, the train guard, informed the Lord Mayor that he knew all the defendants in the dock but did not, however, know Agar. He said that he saw Pierce in the company of another man, looking at the steamboat, in Folkestone in 1854.[18] He saw them together on four or five occasions. He was also working as a guard on the 7.30 p.m. train from Dover in May 1855 and one evening saw Tester standing on the 'up' platform at Reigate. He noticed that Tester was carrying a 'black leather bag ... 12 or 15 inches long'.[19] He later saw him in a First Class carriage. He was also asked about the question of being assigned to the same train for more than one month at a time, which had happened in May 1855 due to Tester's alteration of the guards' work roster. He said that this had not alerted him to anything unusual at the time: 'It is a common thing for guards to be attached to the same train for two consecutive months. This has happened with me two or three times ... I myself have been on one train for as long a period as a year and eight months at a time.'[20] The train to which he had been assigned for that very long period was, he said, the tidal train. Jones was then asked whether reading the newspapers and hearing so much about this infamous robbery had influenced his evidence in any way. He was adamant that it had not: 'I have read an account of these proceedings in the newspapers. I read some portions of Agar's evidence; others I left unread. This, however, has not assisted me to recollect having seen Tester in the month of May. It certainly has not confused my memory.'[21] Jones's slightly impertinent reply elicited laughter in the courtroom.

Booking clerk Frederick Russell, night-watchman John Perry and superintendent John Peake Knight – all from London Bridge station – were called to give evidence. Russell and Perry told of Tester coming into their booking-office one night in May 1855 with that suspicious looking black bag. Knight disagreed with what Jones had said regarding the guards' roster. He said that he did find it unusual for a guard to be working on the same train for more than a month: 'If Jones has sworn that he was continued on one train for 20 consecutive months, I should say he must have made a mistake, as the guards do not work the tidal train for consecutive months.'[22] Jones was then recalled and had to admit that, although he had been assigned to work on that one particular train for twenty months, it was 'unusual' and 'not very common' for this to happen.[23]

Edward Natali Francis, a partner at the firm of Edgington & Co., based at Duke Street, London, was called to talk about a sum of £600 that was paid out from the Bank of England in the name of 'Edgington' on 28 May 1855. He was able to confirm that no such legitimate transaction had taken place on behalf of his company that day.[24] The press described the next witness; Inspector Frederick Williamson of the Metropolitan Police; as having 'been engaged with Sergeant Smith in assisting to unravel the mysteries connected with the robbery'.[25] 'Dolly' Williamson, as he was known, told the court how he had 'accompanied Mr Rees, the solicitor for the prosecution, to Pierce's house, and found there the Turkish bonds, three documents relating to the lease of a house ... some other papers ... a gold watch and chain ... three seals, two leather straps, a box containing tools, and two trunks'.[26]

With that, witness testimonies came to an end. It was now the responsibility of the Lord Mayor to consider all that he had seen and heard over the past few weeks, and to come to a determination about whether there was enough credible evidence to justify sending the prisoners to trial. The proceedings were adjourned to allow him to consider the matter.

CHAPTER 16

A Case to Answer

———•———

Pierce, Burgess and Tester were brought before the Lord Mayor again on Saturday, 20 December 1856. Even though the purpose of the short sitting was merely to fulfill the legal requirement of remanding the alleged train robbers until the following Wednesday, a 'great crowd assembled at the gates of the Mansion House' hoping to catch a glimpse of them.[1] Wontner used the opportunity to apply, on behalf of Pierce, for the return of certain documents that had been confiscated from his client's house by the police. These documents had, he claimed, 'nothing whatever to do with the charge against his client....'[2] The application was refused by the Lord Mayor who said that it should be left to the discretion of Rees what papers to detain. Buchanan made the rather poignant request that his client, Tester, be permitted to speak with his father, 'a most respectable man', at Newgate Prison.[3] He said that this conversation would only take place through the bars and with the governor of Newgate present. The Lord Mayor, however, said that he could do nothing for him: 'The established regulations of the prison cannot be violated in favour of any of the prisoners. If there appears to be any ground for making the application, the visiting magistrates, who can alone interfere, must be appealed to.'[4] The short session over, Pierce, Burgess and Tester were transported back to Newgate to await what would be their final day at the Mansion House.

That final day before the Lord Mayor took place on Wednesday, 24 December 1856. Once the 'voluminous depositions of the witnesses' had been read out by Mr Goodman, the chief clerk, Chapman was recalled to clarify some still outstanding details about the keys.[5] He was questioned by Lewis about whether he and his colleagues had been careless with the keys in their possession:

> Lewis: Did you hear of frequent complaints of those being mislaid?
> Chapman: I cannot say that I did.
> Lewis: Do you mean to swear that you had not frequent complaints of the key of the bullion room being mislaid?
> Chapman: I cannot say I have heard complaints. I have heard of the key being mislaid.
> Lewis: Have you heard complaints made four or five times of the keys being mislaid?
> Chapman: I should say not.
> Lewis: Have the keys been found at times on the pier or on the harbour?
> Chapman: Not that I am aware of.
> Lewis: Have you never heard of that?
> Chapman: Not that I am aware of.
> Lewis: For how long at a time have the keys been missing – many days at a time?
> Chapman: I should say not five minutes.
> Lewis: Then what gave rise to complaints?
> Chapman: I have heard of no complaints – I merely heard the remark, 'Where are my keys?'
> Lewis: Did you never hear of their being missed for several days together?
> Lewis: No; Certainly not....[6]

Fanny was also recalled to clarify how well she was acquainted with Tester. She said that she had known him when he was a clerk in the superintendent's office at Tunbridge station.

The presentation of the evidence at the Mansion House was now finally at an end and it was time for the Lord Mayor to announce his decision. The beliefs and hopes of the prisoners were dashed when he declared that the evidence against them was sufficiently strong to warrant sending them for trial at the next session of the Central Criminal Court. They were duly remanded in custody.[7] Before they were led away, the Lord Mayor asked whether they had anything to say in their defence. Burgess and Tester both said simply, 'I am not guilty', while Pierce remarked: 'I have nothing to say. I reserve my defence.'[8]

This brought the first act of this judicial theatre to an end. The examination before the Lord Mayor had engendered huge interest among the general public and there was no reason to believe that the forthcoming trial at the Old Bailey would be any different. Throughout the examination many were sceptical about what Agar's motivation had been for agreeing to give evidence and there were those who wondered if his real aim had been to facilitate an escape while being transported to the Mansion House. On at least one occasion this rumour was given enough credence to cause the normal routine of the prison authorities to be altered:

'... the usual plan of simply sending down a cab to fetch Agar from the Penitentiary at Milbank [SIC], was departed from, and instead, the police van was dispatched for his conveyance, the whole of the other cells of which were filled with policemen, so that if any rescue had been attempted, it could have been easily prevented. Upon the arrival of the van at the Mansion-house, instead of coming up at the usual entrance for prisoners, it drew up before the private entrance to the Lord Mayor's residence....'[9]

In the end, though, no such escape attempt was made and Agar would get the opportunity of telling his story all over again, this time before the judges of the Old Bailey. The outcome for the defendants on that next occasion would be even more

significant. In a sense they had failed this first test of their innocence. The Lord Mayor was convinced that Agar's evidence,
along with the collaboration of the other witnesses, was credible
enough to conclude that there was a case to answer. Still, this
was no guarantee that a conviction would be handed down at
the Old Bailey. Agar's character and the quality of his evidence
would have to be assessed all over again. On that basis there
were many who still doubted that anyone would ever be
convicted of this crime.

CHAPTER 17

Jim the Penman

———•———

One unexpected effect of Agar's decision to give evidence regarding the train robbery was the consequence it had for the major London crime gang led by Saward. When Agar mentioned the name of his criminal associate at the Mansion House, he was shining a light into a dark area of London crime about which most people knew very little. The newspapers soon picked up on this: '... the amazing Bullion Robbery links itself with the marvellous tale of the Forged Cheques ... the hero common to both transactions being "Jem Saward the Barrister" alias "the Penman", or to speak of so great a man with becoming respect, James Saward, Esq., Barrister-at-Law and Special Pleader, of the Inner Temple and Home Circuit.'[1]

Agar's mention of Saward at the Mansion House was not a casual or unplanned event, even though he might have tried to make it appear so. The revelation came about when he was questioned directly by Bodkin, the prosecution lawyer, regarding the sale of the newly sized bars of gold:[2]

Bodkin: To whom did you sell them?
Agar: I made an appointment to meet a person, and I sold them to him.
Bodkin: Where did you meet that person?
Agar: I met him at Dalston.
Bodkin: Do you know that person's name?
Agar: Yes.

Bodkin: You had better state it.

Agar: I think it is not to be named at present; at least, I have
no objection to name it if it is right. Of course there was a
great part of the gold left when I was arrested that was not
sold, and probably that party may have purchased the
remainder.

This comment seemed to suggest that Agar resented the fact that
Saward, along with Pierce, was still making considerable money
out of the stolen gold while he was behind bars.

Bodkin: I do not know why there should be any concealment
about it; give us the name.

At this the Lord Mayor interrupted and said that he thought 'the
name should be given'. Agar then gave the name, although the
pressure applied to him could hardly be described as arm
twisting, especially when one considers how vehemently he
refused to answer earlier questions put to him about his old
accomplice Nash.

Agar: The person I sold it to is named James Saward.
Bodkin: What is he, do you know?
Agar: Well, he is termed a barrister.

This answer was greeted with laughter from the public. Lewis
referred to 'a gang called the Saward gang' and its existence was
confirmed by Agar. It was clear that Agar had been telling the
authorities a lot about the activities of Saward and his criminal
associates. He knew practically everything about them, having
worked for and with Saward for years. At that time most citizens
were unaware of the scale of forgery that was being perpetrated
in London – much of it by Saward and Agar: 'The public would
hardly credit the enormous amount of fraud practised upon the
bankers of the metropolis by means of forgery, and the extraordinary and ingenious devices that are resorted to for the purpose

of obtaining genuine signatures of persons of responsibility, with a view to their being afterwards made use of for the purposes of forgery.'[3]

Agar had now made public the amazing life being led by Mr James Townsend Saward, barrister and 'pigeon fancier'. The ingenuity of Saward's operation was that he seemed, to all appearances, an honest and respectable barrister. He was around fifty years of age and had been called to the bar in 1841. He had chambers at 4 Hare Court, Temple. He was known by many as the well-dressed man who resided in style at Villa House, Walworth. Yet, in reality, he was a dangerous, leading figure in the criminal underworld inhabited by people such as Edward Agar and William Pierce.

The authorities had been working hard for some time to prosecute those responsible for bank fraud in London, as was evidenced by Agar's own arrest. They enjoyed some success against Saward's underlings, two of whom were called William Salt Hardwicke and Henry Attwell.[4] The authorities' investigations were revealing the complicated and well-planned criminal scams that people like Saward and Agar were capable of running.

Hardwicke was a seasoned criminal of sixty-two years of age who lived with his wife at 20 Nelson Square, Blackfriars Road, where they rented lodgings from a Mr and Mrs Meek. Hardwicke had been a criminal acquaintance of Saward's for over twenty years.[5] In fact, his association with Saward had already got him into considerable trouble. On one occasion he only escaped being tried for his criminal activity by resorting to bribery. According to his wife, she gave 'someone belonging to the gaol' an amount of money and he was let go.[6] Eventually, however, the law caught up with him and in 1837 he was convicted of larceny and sentenced to transportation for seven years. Because of this conviction he felt some bitterness towards Saward, and when he met him again after returning to England he told him so: '... From the manner in which you treated me,' he said, 'I never intended to call upon you again.'[7] It did not take long, however, for Saward to work his charm on Hardwicke once more: '... never mind, old fellow,' he told him, 'we will pay up all arrears, and we will go together, and get some money.'[8] Before long Hardwicke was once again involved in Saward's world of serious crime.

Attwell was only in his early twenties and relatively new to the world of serious crime. When he first met Saward he lived in Cottage Lane under the name of Hawkes with a woman called Elizabeth Evans who was posing as his wife. He was first introduced to Saward through a third party when he came into the possession of two blank cheques and three cancelled cheques from a burglary in Spitalfields and was trying to figure out what to do with them.[9] He was pointed in the direction of Saward, who told him that the blank cheques should be forged, using the writing on the cancelled cheques as a guide, and that someone should then be sent to the bank to cash them. It was the same method as that used by Agar, undoubtedly because Agar had worked so closely with Saward. Attwell agreed to the scheme, and Saward went ahead and set it in motion.

A central figure in Saward's gang was James Anderson. According to Attwell, Saward called Anderson his 'sender', which was a reference to the way he sent unwitting people to the bank to cash the forged cheques.[10] Saward himself did all the forging. Just like Agar, Anderson would recruit an innocent person to go to the bank, by answering advertisements placed in newspapers by people looking for work. Attwell was sent to the Bank of Barclay, Bevan, Tritton & Co., in Lombard Street to watch one of these men, a Mr Maudesley Draper, cash one of the stolen cheques that he had provided.[11] Everything went smoothly on that occasion and the money was paid out. Saward later exchanged the notes for gold and they all shared in the proceeds. Attwell's other cheque was dealt with in a similar manner, all under Saward's close supervision. After this, Attwell began to work frequently with Saward all over London on his various scams involving stolen and forged cheques.

One of their acts of forgery was perpetrated upon a London solicitor named Alfred Turner, who was based at Red Lion Square. Once again the operation was planned and supervised by Mr Saward. The first step was accomplished when Turner's pocketbook was stolen in March 1856. He felt sure that it contained at least one blank cheque at the time, along with a confidential letter from a client that, conveniently for the thieves, included Turner's name and address.[12] Next Saward needed a sample of Turner's handwriting in order to forge the cheque so, in April 1856, Attwell turned up at Turner's office posing as a new client called Mr Hunter. Cleverly, Saward had told him to use this name so that they could get Turner to write 'Hun', the first three letters of the word 'hundred'.[13] Attwell was dealt with by Turner's clerk, Robert Wilson. Along with the false name, Attwell gave Wilson an address at Pakenham Street, Gray's Inn Road. He asked that Wilson write a letter on his behalf to a Mr Hesp of 58 Charrington Street, Oakley Square, requesting payment of an IOU in the amount of £38 18s 6d. Everything seemed to be above board and Wilson had no reason to be suspicious of this new client. He made the application for the money. They encountered no problems and a 'genteel-looking young man' soon arrived at the solicitor's office and settled the full debt in gold.[14] This young man was, in reality, Attwell's brother, sent there with gold supplied by Attwell himself.[15] Mr Turner happened to be there when the young man came in and he took the gold from him and handed it over to Wilson. A few days later Attwell, alias Mr Hunter, arrived at the office to collect his money. The problem was that Wilson paid him in cash, which was of no help to Saward in carrying out the forgery.

As the gang still needed a cheque with sample handwriting on it, they were left with no other option but to try again. This time they decided to use a larger amount of money and leave it in Turner's possession for a longer period of time, so that he would deposit it in a bank. On 19 June Attwell paid his next visit to Turner's office. On this occasion he said he wanted a letter written to a Mr Hart of 6 Melton Street, Euston Square, demanding payment of another IOU. The amount owed to him this time, he said, was £103 15s 6d.[16] Once again they did as requested and, just as before, in 'a day or two' the IOU was settled in full when a man came in and paid with a £50 note and the balance in gold. The money was deposited to Turner's account at Gosling's Bank in Fleet Street. Attwell arrived to collect his money on 14 June and Wilson filled up a cheque for him, which he got Turner to sign. Wilson got Attwell to sign a receipt for the cheque, which he signed as 'H. Hunter'.[17] As Turner was in the office, he got a look at his new client, Mr Hunter.

As usual the gang had covered their tracks with extreme care. They wanted to make sure that these letters requesting payment of the IOUs would not fall into the wrong hands. So, on 1 April, a man who gave the name of Mr Hesp had arrived at 58 Charrington Street, Oakley Square. He rented a room from the owner, Elizabeth Shoebrook. She informed him that the rent would be six shillings a week and he paid her a two-shilling deposit. He then said that he was going out of town until the following Thursday and asked her to take in his luggage for him, if it arrived, and any letters addressed to him. On Thursday he arrived back at the house, went to his room, took the two letters that had arrived and left. He never returned. A similar event occurred at the house of Eliza Brewer – 6 Melton Street, Euston Square – in June. This time the man gave his name as Mr Hart. He also collected his letters and disappeared. According to Eliza Brewer: '... he never slept in the room or occupied it'.[18]

Now that Saward had a sample cheque to work with, he could get on with forging the handwriting styles of both Wilson, who wrote the cheques, and Turner, who signed them. When Turner's blank cheque had been filled out, the next step was to get someone to present it at a bank. This was the riskiest part of the scam and was the responsibility of Saward's associate, Anderson. As usual, an innocent party was found to perform the task. William Hardy, with an address at 7 Euston Mews, Euston Square, innocently placed an advertisement in *The Times* seeking employment and, although he did not know it yet, was about to be dragged unwittingly into the crime of cheque fraud. Hardy had recently left a position with a Colonel Portlock of Woolwich and was delighted to be called to meet a 'Mr Taylor' at 76 Prince Albert Road, Regent's Park, with a view, he thought, to gaining a position as 'an under clerk'.[19] 'Mr Taylor' was, in reality, Anderson and he offered Hardy the position for a guinea a week. Hardy gladly accepted his offer and agreed to meet his new employer again at the University Hotel, Tottenham Court Road, the following day. They met in the coffee room, as arranged, and 'Mr Taylor' gave Hardy the cheque to cash for him in the amount of £410 7s 4d. 'Mr Taylor' told him to ask for it in eight £50 notes and the rest in gold, and then to bring it to the address on Prince Albert Road where they had met on the previous day. Hardy was about to unwittingly cash a cheque that had been forged on Turner's account.

On that day, 28 June 1856, Augustus Bailey Bushnell was working at his job as a cashier at Gosling's Bank when Hardy came in to cash the cheque. Just as Bushnell was trying to effect the transaction, Hardwicke arrived on the scene and, to distract the cashier, repeatedly interrupted him by asking questions about where a certain Mr Richards could be located. Bushnell, who found him most annoying, tried unsuccessfully to get him to wait until he had finished serving his customer. Hardy received the £410 7s 4d from Bushnell and left the bank. He walked towards Prince Albert Road to deliver the money to his employer, but instead met Anderson, alias Mr Taylor, on his way at Mornington Crescent. Hardy handed over the money and Anderson told him that he was taking the next train to Liverpool. He gave Hardy half a sovereign and said he would be in touch when he returned. Hardy never heard from his new employer again.[20]

This was not the end of the scam: Saward's operations were too sophisticated for that. The criminals knew that there was a good chance that the bank had kept a record of the numbers printed on the notes that they had handed out to Hardy. These would be checked once Turner missed the money from his account and it was realized that a crime had been committed. Therefore they had to find a safe way to exchange the notes. They had learned their lesson from the arrest of Agar's accomplice, William Nash. The operation was so well planned that it next extended its reach to Germany. On 2 July 1856, Hardwicke's wife went into the Temple Bar branch of the Union Bank of London and arranged for £20 to be sent to a Mr Richard Gurney in Hamburg. John Beattie, the manager, handled the transaction for her himself and she gave her name as Mrs Wilson of High Street, Woolwich.

On 5 July, Hardwicke and Attwell called into the bankers, Messrs Stressau, in Hamburg. Hardwicke presented his draft for £20 and was paid the amount in a mixture of French gold and Hamburg currency.[21] He signed for it in the name: 'R. Gurney'. Having thereby proved his credentials as a bone fide customer, he then asked the bank officials if they could change some money for him. They agreed, and he took four £50 notes from his pocket and Attwell provided four more. When checked later, the numbers on the notes taken in Hamburg that day showed them to be the same notes that the gang had swindled out of Turner's account in London. This exchange of the money for the 'clean' £400 in Germany marked the successful culmination of the intricate and well-planned theft from Turner's account. It was only one of many such frauds that the Saward gang managed to carry out successfully.

Although they had enjoyed great success, by September 1856 Hardwicke and Attwell's fruitful period was about to come to an end. Saward and his associates had managed to come into the possession of a number of stolen blank cheques from solicitors in the Great Yarmouth area and, as usual, they set about getting handwriting samples from the owners. On 30 August 1856, Attwell called on the legal practice of Charles Henry Chamberlain, in Great Yarmouth, using the name Attwood. He said that he needed Chamberlain to collect a debt of £104 3s 5d for him from an Edward Dixon of 18 Compton Street, London.[22] Attwell, knowing that a detailed story always sounded more convincing, told Chamberlain that 'Mr Dixon was one of those sort of persons who never would pay his debts unless under some sort of pressure....'[23] Chamberlain agreed to write a letter for him and Attwell gave his address as the Angel Inn, Great Yarmouth. On the same day Attwell visited Charles John Palmer of Messrs Reynolds Palmer. Again he used the name Attwood and this time asked that a debt be collected from a gentleman called William Jones of 13 Union Terrace, Bagnigge Wells Road, London. The amount owed to him, he said, was £105 14s. When Palmer asked about the particulars of the debt the client did seem a bit vague, only saying that it was 'partly for goods sold, and partly for money lent'.[24] Nevertheless, Palmer wrote for the money. On 1 September it was the turn of Henry Blake Miller, of Messrs Miller, Son & Bugg, based at Norwich. Once again Attwell asked that a debt be collected, but this time he called himself Henry Cornwall. The amount due he again said was £105 14s and 'Mr Jones of Bagnigge Wells Road in London' was again the imaginary debtor. Miller agreed to represent him.

In all three cases the solicitors had no difficulty in collecting the debts due. However, this time the criminals' luck was about to run out. The solicitors were in contact with one another and communications that Chamberlain had had with some of his colleagues led to him becoming suspicious. He decided to inform the authorities. It was just the kind of tip-off they were waiting for. When he met Chamberlain on the 15 September 1856, Attwell was taken into custody. Two IOUs were found on him and, at his lodgings, letters written by three different solicitors. On 26 September, Robert Wilson from Alfred Turner's legal practice in London was brought to Yarmouth, and he identified Attwell as the man who had called himself Mr Hunter.[25] This all led them to Hardwicke and at *his* lodgings, among other incriminating items, police found a £1,000 exchequer bill and a pistol. Hardwicke's wife was also arrested in London. Mr Beattie, the manager of the Temple Bar branch of the Union Bank of London, identified her as the Mrs Wilson who arranged for the money to be sent to Hamburg.

Richard Mullens, the solicitor to the associated bankers of the City of London, who had already brought about the arrest and conviction of Edward Agar for forgery, travelled down to Great Yarmouth to see the prisoners. Hardwicke had a frank discussion with Mullens and asked him if he could arrange to have his wife released, as she had only gone to the Union Bank that day 'by his direction' and was not involved in any crime.[26] She did, of course, know that she was giving a false name in the bank that day and she must have known that some illegality was afoot. Nevertheless, perhaps in return for being free with information about those at the top of the gang, Mullens acceded to Hardwicke's request and his wife was released. One of the things Hardwicke admitted to the investigators was that, through Saward, he was acquainted with Agar.[27]

Towards the end of 1856, as they now had Attwell and Hardwicke in custody and co-operating, and were also getting information from Agar, the authorities were ready to move against Saward. Firstly his activities were openly exposed by Agar in his testimony at the Mansion House. Then Saward was arrested by two police officers called Huggett and Moss at 9 John Street, Oxford Street on 26 December, 1856.[28] At first Saward denied that he was the man they sought. They charged him with 'being concerned with Hardwicke, Attwell, and Anderson' in forgery.[29] He denied any knowledge of these names: 'I do not know such people,' he said. 'I never saw them in my life, nor do I know anything respecting the forgery.'[30] However, when he was searched, the officers found two blank cheques in his pocket. According to Huggett and Moss, it was only when they forced him to accompany them to the police station that he finally relented and admitted that he was Jim Saward.[31]

Saward and his assistant James Anderson were brought before an examination at the Mansion House in January, 1857. Although the authorities had evidence pertaining to a great many frauds and forgeries, they decided to choose one on which to prosecute the two criminals:

James Anderson, Freehold Street, Durham Road, Hoxton, servant, for forging and uttering on the 14th of June, 1856, a bill of exchange for £1,000, with intent to defraud Messrs. Heywood, Kennard, and Co., bankers, 4, Lombard Street.
James Townsend Saward, Villa House, Walworth Common, Barrister-at-Law, on suspicion of being concerned with the above James Anderson in forging and uttering the said bill of exchange for £1,000.

Mullens, the solicitor for the banks, informed the Lord Mayor that although 'he intended to make the cheques alluded to on the last occasion the basis of the charges against the prisoners', he would also 'give evidence of other forgeries....'[32] Until Agar's evidence at the Mansion House, most people had never heard of Saward, but now his arrest was a big story: 'On Friday afternoon Seward [sic] ... was brought up in custody before the Lord Mayor, charged with being concerned, with another person named Anderson, in forging and uttering a bill of exchange for 1000*l.* , on the 14th of June last, with intent to defraud Messrs. Kennard and Heywood, bankers in Lombard-street.'[33]

Having remained at large for so long, it is ironic that the criminal lives of both Agar and Saward were being exposed to the public at the same time:

While the Lord Mayor was proceeding with the business in the Justice-room at the Mansion-house, on the 26th ... intelligence was brought to his lordship that James Townsend Saward, the 'barrister' alluded to in the proceedings against Pierce, Burgess and Tester ... was in the custody of Huggett, the City detective officer, and would be put to the bar at the close of the ordinary list of prisoners. At half-past three o'clock Saward was brought before the Lord Mayor. He is a very intelligent-looking man, apparently about 50 years of age. He was in a state of perfect self-possession, and uttered the few words he spoke in a confident and unembarrassed tone. Before the examination was commenced it was known that the prisoner had been apprehended, not for any participation he was supposed to have had in the gold ... robbery, but for the forgery of a bill of exchange for £1,000, in which offence two convicts are said to have been his accomplices....'[34]

Saward's reputation as a criminal mastermind was soon obvious for all to see:

> Mathematicians speak of the beautiful solution of a question, and often call a formula or proposition elegant. Mr Saward appears to us to have solved the attractive problem of appropriating to himself a sum of money in a banker's custody, without the consent or knowledge of the party in whose name the balance stands, with a nicety, a dexterity, a subtlety, and fecundity of device, than which we can conceive no prettier process in geometry or algebra.[35]

The main evidence in the trial of Saward and Anderson would be the testimonies of Attwell and Hardwicke. They were able to provide details of a catalogue of forgery scams in which they had been involved under Saward's supervision. They could give dates, places and names, all of which would be very damaging to Saward and Anderson's defence. But, in addition to the evidence provided by Attwell and Hardwicke, a whole series of other witnesses were willing to give evidence: the stooges used to cash the forged cheques; the landladies of premises used for false addresses; and the many bankers and account holders who had been deceived. Many people felt angry that Saward, so obviously a serious criminal, had been able to live a double life as a barrister:

> The question is properly asked, How did 'Jem Saward,' who figures in the 'great city forgeries,' get to the bar? ... He has been for a long time the associate of thieves. Who is he? By what two barristers was he proposed? By whom of the Benchers approved? For without this preliminary certificate of character admission of a student is impracticable. The Inner

Temple boasts of a sort of preliminary classical examination. Was 'Jem Saward' subjected to this? These are questions which the society has a right to ask, and the proposers might properly be called upon to state what was their knowledge of him.[36]

Many wondered, but for Agar's willingness to talk, would Saward ever have been called to answer for his crimes? The Lord Mayor determined that Saward and Anderson should be sent for trial at the Old Bailey. Before their fates could be decided on, however, the case of the Great Train Robbery awaited adjudication.

CHAPTER 18

Cover-up

———•———

A s the examination of the case against Pierce, Burgess and
Tester was taking place before the Lord Mayor at the
Mansion House in November 1856, a rather shocking report
emerged. It was stated that, contrary to widespread belief, the
initial investigation into the Great Train Robbery had not actually been a complete failure. According to this revelation, a few
weeks after the robbery, the Metropolitan Police – or 'the City
Detectives' as they were called – had been able to confirm for
the South Eastern Railway that the robbery had been
committed on their line between London and Dover and,
furthermore, it was claimed that they had been able to provide
the names of the culprits involved: 'On the receipt of telegraphic
news from Paris, announcing the robbery, the city detectives
were called upon to act in the matter, and within a few weeks
after the occurrence they were enabled to inform the directors
that the robbery had been committed on their line, between
London and Dover, by Agar and his three accomplices....[1]
According to this report, and the rumours that accompanied it,
the authorities had known practically everything from early on:
'With the exception of a few incidents detailed by Agar, the
police had acquired all the principal facts, and a report was
presented to the directors, which if it had at once been acted
upon the whole of the prisoners would have been taken, and
probably also the receivers, and a large amount of the stolen
treasure recovered.'[2]

This was sensational news. Could it be true that the police and the South Eastern Railway Company had known all along what had happened on that night in May 1855 and had failed to act? When one looks at the investigation of the crime there are a number of troubling questions. Why had so many pieces of information been seemingly overlooked or neglected? A number of witnesses to relevant events on the night of the robbery were either not interviewed, or their evidence was ignored or, at least in one case, they were asked to say nothing about what they knew. For example, there had been numerous suspicious sightings of all the robbers at Folkestone in the months leading up to the crime, yet none of those sightings was pursued vigorously. As soon as he heard about the robbery, Inspector Hazel told the investigating police and the railway authorities about the suspicious activities of Pierce and another man he had seen there on a number of occasions. He also told how he saw that other man, who was Agar, in company with Tester. A week or two after the robbery he did meet with a detective, who had authority from the railway company to investigate the crime, and told him everything. But then, amazingly, Hazel received a very strange order: 'I received directions from him to keep quiet what I knew.'[3]

The reason Hazel was given for this bizarre request was 'for fear it should frustrate the ends of justice'.[4] Obviously disturbed by this request to withhold evidence, Hazel also told his story to Captain Barlow, who was managing the company at that time, and he too directed him to keep quiet about it. As far as he could remember, that all happened about a month or so after the robbery. Hazel did as he was ordered and remained silent about the suspicious sightings at Folkestone – until he was asked to talk at the Mansion House.

Superintendent Steer had also seen Agar, Pierce and Burgess in Folkestone. Hazel told the investigators that Steer had also seen them but yet no effort was made to interview him at all: strange, since he was such a high ranking policeman at Folkestone. Steer said at the Mansion House: 'I have not been examined in this matter by anybody. When I heard of the robbery I made no special report of this circumstance. In common conversation it had been spoken of to the railway people. I made no specific report to any one....'[5] Neither Hazel nor Steer got to go public about what they knew until Fanny Kay made her revelations. Only then were they interviewed by John Rees, and subsequently called as witnesses before the Lord Mayor.

Charles Chapman of the harbour office in Folkestone said that he was not asked about Agar coming down to collect that package of money in October 1854 until 'two or three days' before the proceedings at the Mansion House: 'I cannot remember that any inquiry was made of me at the time the robbery was discovered,' he said.[6] Had Hazel's information been followed up on, it would surely have led the investigators to Chapman and his story of this package sent by rail from London for the man who called himself 'Mr ER Archer'. This would, in turn, have led them on to the information of Sharman and Ledger regarding Agar hanging around Folkestone.

Usually, one of the first things someone investigating a crime of this sort considers is how the culprits managed to get away from the scene of the crime. All forms of possible escape would be considered and investigated. It would be sensible to wonder if the person or persons who stole the valuables that night had escaped to London on board one of the trains out of Dover station. Yet none of the staff on duty at Dover station that night were asked if any suspicious characters had passed through their station. Had they been asked, Williams and Witherden could have told the investigators about the two suspicious men who boarded the 2 a.m. London train. It was reported that, only when Agar was in custody for forgery, was Witherden brought to the Mansion House cells to see him and he identified him as one of two men who boarded a train for London that night carrying heavy bags. Even then the South Eastern Railway Company did not move quickly to have anyone arrested:

... Witherden was taken to the Mansion House lock-up, and among a batch of other prisoners pointed Agar out to the police as one of the men whom he saw get into the mail train at Dover with very heavy bags on the night of the robbery. At this time the company were urged to prosecute, as the police had full knowledge of the receivers, but for some reason they declined doing so.[7]

Neither did any of the investigators delve into the sightings of these men as they disembarked from the train at London Bridge station that morning. Dickenson, the porter at the station, said that as soon as he heard about the robbery he told the railway authorities, namely Weatherhead, the stationmaster, about these two men. He did so, he said, '... the day, or the day but one, after the robbery'.[8] Yet, he heard no more about it. The fact that he saw these two men disembarking from the Dover to London train that night and they refused his help in getting a cab did not seem, perhaps, highly significant, but put together with other information it could well have been.

As one would expect, once it was accepted that the train had been robbed en route to Folkestone, both of the guards on duty that night, Burgess and Kennedy, came under scrutiny. Despite the fact that there were grave doubts about Burgess's involvement almost from the beginning, nothing was done about him and he remained an employee of the company until arrested. The railway later claimed that he was put under a 'searching interrogation by the company's officers' at the time of the robbery but, apart from admitting that he sometimes allowed 'gents' to ride illegally in his van, he asserted his innocence.[9] He was also kept under surveillance for a number of months but, apparently, nothing interesting was discovered. He was never seen in the company of either Pierce or Agar during that time. He was seen talking to Tester but this would be in the normal course of their work.[10] That he had been with the company for a considerable length of time, thirteen years, and had no convictions of any sort, were later cited as reasons for not moving against him. The company had, it claimed, 'unlimited confidence' in him.[11] 'Confidence was placed in him, and although there have been

reasons for some time strongly to suspect that he was a partici-
pator in this great robbery, it was not thought prudent to
intimate any suspicion of that sort to him by removing him from
the situation that he held.'[12] It is troubling that Rees claimed to
have lost the written account he had made of his interview with
Burgess around Good Friday of 1856.[13] He also, of course,
denied the claim made by Burgess that he had offered him a deal
in return for immunity from prosecution.[14]

There are also a number of remarkable features relating to the
railway company's treatment of Tester. On examination of the
facts, his obvious alteration of the guards' roster would have
struck anyone as being suspicious. It was also common knowledge that he had access to at least one of the keys to the safes.
Furthermore, it emerged that when he was interrogated the
detectives did find glaring holes in his story:

> ... the detectives who were employed by the company ... and
> others, had ascertained that ... [Tester] had been in company
> with suspicious characters at Folkestone, and had dined at the
> pavilion with one of them ... Tester was highly indignant that
> he should be suspected, and stoutly denied having dined with
> any stranger there; when, however, he was cautioned, and
> assured that there could be no mistake about the matter, he
> admitted dining with a party. At first he did not remember the
> stranger's name; then he recollected, when pressed, that it was
> a friend named Coningham [sic], or Adams. But could give no
> account as to where he lived, or how long he (Tester) had been
> acquainted with him.'[15]

It is clear that the South Eastern Railway Company did not want
their employee arrested. He decided to move to Sweden. We
have to wonder if he did so because many of his workmates in
London knew of, or at least suspected, his involvement in the
robbery, and relations with them had become strained. Even
worse for the railway company was the fact that he received
glowing testimonials from his employers before he left, including

one from Samuel Smiles, the secretary of the company. It is difficult to accept that Smiles would not have been at least suspicious
about Tester's role in the robbery. Smiles would later have to
explain his actions and his defence was that he simply did not
know Tester at all:

> I was requested by Mr Tester, the assistant-superintendent in
> the passenger manager's office to furnish him with a certificate
> of character on his leaving the company's service, to assume
> the position of General Manager of the Royal Swedish
> Railway. I did not know Mr Tester, but was informed by his
> chief that he had been a faithful servant, and that I might give
> him the certificate of character which he requested.

After Fanny told her story it became known that Tester had
been seen a number of times on one particular night in May with
that suspicious black bag, but this had not been previously
exposed by the investigators. Stephen Jones, the guard, saw him
at Reigate station around 9.25 p.m. that evening.[16] Jones knew
him well 'as a person in the employment of the company' and he
saw him 'coming out of the refreshment room door, on the up
side' carrying that bag.[17] Jones later saw him enter a First Class
carriage heading for London. Yet Jones said that he had not
been asked about any of this: I did not ... mention about seeing
Tester with the black bag in May, because I was not asked the
question ... I was never asked about it before – what I was asked
about in June was, if I had seen Pierce at Folkestone – I do not
remember that I was asked anything else at that time.[18]

Fredrick Russell and John Perry, the booking clerk and the
night-watchman at London Bridge station, also had information
to impart regarding Tester and that bag. Tester had been in
Russell's office and Perry had actually lifted the bag, but they
were also ignored, until after Fanny's revelations. Perry said that
when they read about Agar's evidence they decided to come
forward themselves with their information: 'I never said
anything about a black bag until I had read it [Agar's evidence];

we had not the least thought of anything of the kind – when we read Agar's evidence it freshened our memories that it was somewhere about the time that the gold robberies took place.'

There was much more evidence that did not come out until the hearing at the Mansion House, including the testimonies of the cab drivers, the staff members from various public houses and the coffee-shop owner, Mr Clements. The hearing at the Mansion House revealed that either the investigation was inept or, as the newspapers asserted, some important information had been covered up and more not pursued at all. Perhaps the authorities would argue that they could not possibly have known about much of this evidence without the detailed information provided by Fanny and Agar, but many people believed that it was only when Fanny insisted on going public with her story that the authorities felt they had to act. Once Fanny and then Agar began to speak, the truth could no longer be hidden and the authorities had to reveal what they knew and follow up on the leads that they had previously ignored.

Why had the South Eastern Railway been so reluctant to act against the individuals who had robbed them? It was claimed by the company that they did not have anyone arrested in the early months because 'they had some misgivings as to the truth of' what the detectives were telling them.[19] Perhaps the company would also argue that, without the testimony of Agar, the case would not have been strong enough to succeed in court. It is more likely, however, that they did not want to act because they found out, early on, that the train robbery was an inside job. Above all else, they were focused on saving the company's reputation and resisting the claims for compensation. Better to allow the perpetrators of the crime to go unpunished, rather than suffer the consequences of the truth coming out. But now, whether anyone at the company wanted it or not, thanks to Fanny and Agar the whole story was about to be revealed in public at the Old Bailey.

CHAPTER 19

The Trial

There was still one more procedural necessity to go through before the case of the Great Train Robbery could be brought to trial. The bills relating to the case were presented to a grand jury at a special session of the Central Criminal Court at 11 a.m. on 12 January 1857. Among those in attendance were the Lord Mayor, the sheriffs and the under-sheriffs. Once the grand jury had returned true bills against Pierce, Burgess and Tester, the way was clear for the trial to take place.

The trial began at the Old Bailey on the following day, Tuesday, 13 January 1857. Agar and Fanny were both present and ready to act as witnesses. Unlike the proceedings at the Mansion House, this time the prosecution had made sure that there was no confusion or delay surrounding Agar's appearance. Agar and Pierce were both around forty years of age at the time, Burgess and Tester thirty-six and twenty-six respectively. Just like when they appeared before the Lord Mayor, none of the three defendants would be accorded the opportunity of giving their version of events in their own words as, legally, prisoners in the dock were not permitted to testify.

Understandably, the trial attracted considerable attention from both the newspapers and the public and, just as there had been at the Mansion House a few weeks earlier, there was a clamour among people to be there in person. Those writing in the newspapers understood the interest: '... the trial ... excited great interest, owing to the daring nature of the robbery, the ingenuity with which it had been planned and executed, the largeness of the sum involved, and the apparent respectability of some of the persons implicated....'[1]

Considering the great interest in the trial, the organisational skills of the under-sheriffs, Alexander Crosley and James Anderton, were applauded: '... the court was at no period of the day inconveniently crowded, and the proceedings were conducted without the slightest interruption or confusion.'[2] This was achieved, in part, by the insistence that no one gain admittance to the courtroom without an official ticket signed by the sheriffs.

At ten o'clock the judges, Mr Baron Martin and Mr Justice Willes, took their places on the bench, joined by the Lord Mayor, Alderman Humphery, Sir F.G. Moon, Mr Sheriff Mechi, Mr Sheriff Keats and the two under-sheriffs. When the three prisoners arrived from Newgate Prison, Burgess was again wearing his railway uniform, while Tester, like Pierce, was dressed in normal attire. *The Times*' correspondent in court that day thought that Tester, the youngest and least experienced of the three, looked more worried than the others and 'evidently felt the nature of his position much more keenly than his colleagues'. Pierce and Burgess, on the other hand, 'appeared to view their position with perfect unconcern', although Pierce's countenance was described as 'sullen'.[3] As the trial got underway, all three defendants were seen to be in frequent communication with their legal representatives and Burgess took notes throughout, handing them to his counsel periodically.

The prosecution was conducted by Mr Serjeant Shee, assisted by Mr Bodkin and Mr Monk. Representing the defendants were: Mr Serjeant Parry, with Mr Ribton, for Pierce; Mr Lewis, with Mr Giffard and Mr Poland, for Burgess; and Mr Serjeant Ballantine, with Mr Sleigh, for Tester. The indictments were read out to the court by Mr Straight, the Clerk of Arraigns, and all three prisoners stood indicted on four counts: the first referred to stealing from 'their masters', the second to 'simple larceny', the third to 'stealing the property in the dwelling house of the company' and the fourth to 'feloniously receiving the same'. When called on, the three defendants pleaded 'not guilty' to all charges.

Shee, in his opening statement for the prosecution, dealt straight away with the publicity that this infamous crime had already engendered and how the jury members would have to deal with that:

> It is scarcely possible that you should not have learnt, through the usual channels of information, the general history of the gold robbery committed upon the South Eastern Railway Company. It is my duty to caution you, however, not to pay the least attention during the course of this inquiry to any information which you may have acquired from that or any other source ... dismiss from your minds everything which up to this period you may have heard relating to the robbery.[4]

He then proceeded to tell the story of the movements of the gold on the night in question:

> Upon that night three boxes containing gold were delivered by their owners to Messrs. Chaplin and Co., the carriers, and by them they were taken to the offices of the South Eastern Railway Company, at London Bridge. One of those boxes contained gold, the property of Messrs. Abel and Co.; another contained gold, the property of Messrs. Spielmann; and the third contained gold, the property of Messrs. Bult ... At Paris it was ascertained that a quantity of shot had been substituted for the gold which those boxes had originally contained, and it was clear, owing to the weights at Boulogne and Paris corresponding, that the robbery could not have been committed between those two places. Every inquiry was, of course, instituted, as soon as the fact of the robbery was made known by communication from Paris, to satisfy the directors and the professional advisers of the South Eastern Railway Company as to the place where the robbery must have been perpetrated

... they arrived at length at the reluctant conviction that the robbery must have been effected ... in the van of the train of which Burgess, the guard, had charge.[5]

He provided some background information on the defendants:

The prisoners at the bar have all been in the service of the South Eastern Railway Company. Burgess was in their service on the night of the robbery, and had been so for 13 years before; Pierce had also been in their service, although he was not so at the date of the robbery. Up to 1850 he had been in their employ as a ticket printer; but in that year he was dismissed from that engagement. He was, however, well acquainted with the officers and servants of the South Eastern Railway Company. Tester, at the date of the robbery, was a clerk in the office of the superintendent of traffic, and he had therefore ample means for obtaining knowledge and information as to the traffic that was conveyed upon the line.[6]

Shee decided to make direct reference to the fact that his main witness, Agar, was not only a convicted felon but had also, by his own admission, been involved in the very robbery regarding which he was about to give evidence:

'... he is now a convict, having been arrested in August, 1855, and convicted in the October following of uttering a forged cheque, knowing it to be forged. He comes before you from Portland hulks, where he is undergoing a portion of his sentence of transportation for life. I need hardly tell you, gentlemen, that a witness presenting himself before a jury under such circumstances, and acknowledging himself to be guilty of the crime with which the other prisoners are charged, is a person whom a jury ought not to believe without strong corroborative evidence.[7]

But, Shee assured the jury, such 'corroborative evidence' was available and he would bring forward 'a great number of respectable witnesses'.[8] These witnesses would be so credible, he claimed, that Agar's evidence would not even be necessary to gain a conviction: '... you will be of [the] opinion that the circumstantial evidence against the prisoners is so strong that it would be sufficient to convict them of the offence ... even if Agar's evidence were not before you.'[9] He told them that he could not inform them of 'what the pursuits of Agar had been previously to the planning and perpetration of this robbery'.[10] The truth was that he did not want to catalogue for them his main witness's life of crime. He went on to describe how Pierce and Agar had planned the train robbery, their trips to Folkestone to gather information and their attempts and eventual success in gaining copies of the keys. He explained the crucial involvement of Burgess and Tester in the crime. Pierce had been confident, he told the jury, that in Tester he had found a willing and useful accomplice: 'He [Pierce] said that he knew a young man named Tester, the prisoner at the bar, who was in the office of the superintendent of traffic on the line, and that no doubt Tester could get possession of the keys for them.'[11]

Shee went through, for his highly attentive audience, the step by step details of the robbery itself and the distribution of the spoils afterwards. He explained to the jury the circumstances that had led to Agar agreeing to give evidence, demonstrating in the process the honourable nature of his witness: '... having been reconciled to Fanny Kay, or entertaining still a kindly feeling for her as the mother of his child, he arranged, when he was arrested that Pierce should take possession of all his property, and should provide for Fanny Kay and his child.'[12] In contrast, he told the jury about Pierce's subsequent treachery: 'Pierce for a time did contribute something to her support, but afterwards he desisted from doing so, and the result was that Fanny Kay was reduced to the greatest distress.'[13]

Pierce's counsel, Parry, felt obliged to object to these emotive comments, arguing that they had nothing at all to do with the matter before the court 'even if ... true'.[14] The judge disagreed. 'It is quite legitimate,' he said, 'the learned counsel is explaining how

Agar came to make this statement.'[15] Parry's acceptance of the judge's decision was not exactly gracious: 'Surely the motives of a man under such circumstances cannot be evidence! However, if your Lordship thinks otherwise, I have not a word to say.'[16]

Shee brought his opening statement to a conclusion by referring to the degree of 'skill, dexterity, perseverance, and ability' that the execution of the crime had demonstrated on behalf of those involved.[17] He lamented the fact that the principals had not used their obvious skills in the achievement of more wholesome aims. Had they been 'employed in a better cause,' he lamented, 'how different might have been the result'.[18]

When it was time to call the main witness to the stand, Agar was clear and direct from the beginning, just as he had been when examined at the Mansion House. He got straight to the point: 'I am one of the persons by whom a robbery of gold was effected in May, 1855, on the South Eastern Railway....' Under questioning, he went through once again, in great detail, the story of the robbery: the planning, how difficult it had been for them to get possession of the keys, the night of the robbery itself, the melting of the gold and the selling of a portion of the proceeds from the crime. The assembled crowd obviously found his evidence gripping and entertaining and they laughed out loud on a number of occasions, such as when he was questioned about his various aliases and replied: 'I answered to any name they chose to call me.'[19] From the beginning his evidence was intended to leave the jury in no doubt about the roles played by Pierce, Burgess and Tester in the robbery. Asked about how he had first met Pierce and whether, at that time, he knew the man to be a rogue, he said that Pierce was introduced to him by two thieves and that they 'at once proceeded to business'.[20]

When they got their chance to question Agar, the strategy employed by the defence counsels was just as it had been at the Mansion House: to emphasize his life as a professional thief and forger and thereby expose him to the jury as an incredible witness. Under questioning, despite being at the time convicted and incarcerated, Agar once again declared himself innocent of ever being a forger. This was probably because he was hoping to be granted a pardon from his conviction for forgery in return for giving evidence, and perhaps it had been put to him that his conviction for forgery might be quashed on the grounds that he had been framed. Yet his efforts to explain how he had earned his living since leaving the only legitimate job he had ever held – at Mr Davis's linen drapers in Chiswell Street, many years before – were unconvincing: 'I was there for four years – that is fourteen years ago probably, it might be twenty years – I could not say positively – I will not venture to say whether or not it was twenty-two years ago – there was not a robbery there while I was there nor shortly after I left, to my knowledge – I have never been in any employment since'.[21] He was cross-examined on the matter of his employment record by the defence lawyers, but refused to be specific:

> Q: You decline to tell ... how you were gaining your liveli
> hood for the three years after you left the linendraper's
> establishment?
> Agar: Yes – I have no particular motive for declining – I
> decline on the ground that I am not bound to answer – I
> will not answer the question unless I am compelled to do
> so – I am not afraid – if I am compelled to do so, I will – I
> am not afraid of the consequences to myself – I am not
> afraid of being subjected to a prosecution – I decline to
> answer....[22]

He tried to convince the court that he had made his living in recent years by means of financial speculation in America:

> I have earned my living by speculating in the United States of
> America, buying various things – I have been to America
> several times – I do not know the date of my first going to
> America – it was not ten years after leaving Mr Davis, probably
> five years – It might be five and it might be three, I cannot say
> – between the time I left Mr Davis and the time of my going to

America I lived on what I had got – I decline answering how I had got it.[23]

The judge, Mr Baron Martin, losing patience with these evasive answers about how he made his living, urged Agar to answer the question directly: 'I don't see why you should not answer the question. You can't put yourself in a worse situation than you are now, except you did something which would render you liable to be hanged.'[24] At this comment from the judge there was laughter in court, but Agar still refused to answer, saying simply: 'I decline to answer any question as to what I did.'[25] His refusal to answer was not, he insisted, because he feared any consequences or prosecutions that may ensue, but because he refused to be 'obliged to tell'.[26]

Parry went on to pursue the issue of his involvement in illegal activities, but Agar continued to be adamant regarding his innocence where forgery was concerned:

I was not engaged in forgeries – I never was engaged in forgeries ... I decline answering how I got my living then – I speculated in America in various things, not in crime – I did not commit robberies whilst I was in America, or pass cheques ... I never presented a forged cheque in my life, nor have caused any to be presented – I can swear that I never committed a forgery, or ever caused a forgery to be committed in my life....[27]

When it was put to him that he had already been convicted of the crime of forgery and was awaiting transportation at the present time, he replied: 'I am perfectly innocent of the charge I was convicted of – I was convicted upon false evidence – I never presented a forged note....'[28] When asked about his connection with the recently arrested barrister, Mr Saward, he admitted the fact. But he also seemed to be trying to distance himself from any involvement in Saward's arrest, perhaps out of fear of reprisals, even though he was the one, during his testimony at the

Mansion House, who had first exposed Saward publicly as a criminal:

> I have known Saward I should say probably six years; it may be longer ... I know not what he is under charge of, I will swear that – I have been in prison ... I do not know that he is arrested – I never knew Saward by any other names than 'barrister Saward' or 'James Saward' – I never had anything to do with him in the way of cheques – I have discounted bills for him – I have not had any transactions with cheques with him.[29]

No doubt he was also thinking of his possible future pardon and wanted to distance himself from Saward's criminality. The questioning then moved on to his making of the keys to the safes:

> Q: You tell us that you filed these keys; what were you origi-
> nally by calling?
> Agar: I can work at almost anything. I worked at jewellery
> and carpentering – I can make jewellery.
> Q: And bars of gold?
> Agar: Well, there is proof of that.[30]

When asked whether these were the first false keys that he had ever made, he replied that he had made some before in order for Pierce to commit a robbery at one of South Eastern's railway stations.[31]

Agar testified that he had known Tester for between three and four years. He told the court of the time he visited Tester at his lodgings in Margate and enjoyed tea with him. To prove this assertion he gave a detailed description of the location of the house in which Tester lived at that time: '... when you went out of the station,' he said, 'you turned to the left and the house faced you. I do not know the name of the place.'[32] He also said that an elderly female, who kept the house, had served them tea in the front parlour, but he did not know her name. He did not sleep there that night, but spent the night instead 'at a public house of the sign of the "Elephant"'. Tester had joined him at that establishment for 'a glass of grog ... in the smoking room'.[33] He also answered questions regarding their meeting at Folkestone, and told how they had walked 'arm in arm' from the upper station. He said that Tester knew him to be a thief from the beginning and that he was even '... introduced to him as such'.[34]

Agar verified that none of the railway employees at Folkestone was involved in the robbery in any way: 'I endeavoured to get the impressions of the keys unknown to the servants down there,' he said: 'none of them knew what I was there for.'[35] He told the court about Thomas Sharman, the clerk at Folkestone station, saying that he did not try to make an accomplice of him. His only aim was to trick the gentleman: 'I got into communication with him, to be familiar with him, and when his back was turned, to get the keys from their place – that was part of the plan between me and Tester....'[36] But he admitted that he had got nowhere with this plan, simply because he could not get on friendly terms with Sharman: '... I could not make any impression upon Sharman ... I could not form any connection with him....'[37]

By the time he had finished giving his evidence, Agar had done his best to convince the jury about the involvement of Pierce, Burgess and Tester in the robbery. His testimony had been clear, cogent, delivered with great confidence, and detailed. Had he not been a convicted criminal, his story would have been unassailable. But as he was a criminal, the corroboration of his evidence by other witnesses would be crucial.

Of those other witnesses, John Chaplin and his bullion porter, Thomas Sellings, were called first. They confirmed their parts in the delivery of the wooden boxes, containing the gold and other valuables, to London Bridge station on the evening of the robbery. Edgar Cox, the clerk, testified that he received the boxes from Chaplin on behalf of the railway company and that they were weighed before being put on the train. Henry Abel confirmed that he had sent six bars of gold on the ill-fated train that evening. He complained about the ungentlemanly behaviour of the South Eastern Railway in not, at first, paying him compensation for his financial loss.[38] He confirmed that they did finally pay him in December 1855.[39] John Bailey, the porter at London Bridge station, said that he remembered Mr Weatherhead, his boss, locking the boxes inside the safes that evening. Later he transported the safes himself to the train from Weatherhead's office and handed them over to Burgess. John Kennedy, the underguard to Burgess that night, was unable to shed any light on how the gold had been stolen. He did hint that Burgess did his best to keep him busy and out of the way while the train was standing at the platform at London Bridge. 'Shortly before the train started,' he explained, 'Burgess asked me to look round the train to see that all was right....[40] He also said that from the time they left London until they arrived in Dover he never saw Burgess once.[41] He testified that he saw Agar 'in company with Burgess at the latter end of April or the beginning of May, 1855, near the London-bridge station, at a public house'. He saw Agar again on the night of the robbery 'on the platform about the time for the departure of the mail train'.[42]

The railway staff from Folkestone were called to give their evidence. Richard Hart, the porter, said that he helped to remove the safes from the train that night and transport them to the harbour. John Spicer, the night-watchman, said that he received them from Hart and 'kept watch over them till morning'.[43] Robert Mackay, the clerk at the telegraph office, was up all that night, he told the jury, and he was sure that the safes did not move during that time. John McNie, the policeman for the South Eastern Railway, also gave his account of what he had experienced. 'I relieved Spicer in charge of the bullion chests on the morning of the 16th May, 1855,' he said, 'and did not lose sight of them until they were placed on board of the boat.'[44]

James Golder, the mate of the Lord Warden steamboat, remembered the safes being put on deck that morning. 'I had my eye on them the whole time,' he said. Golder was also able to give evidence relating to the damaged condition of one of the boxes on its arrival in France: 'When the chests were opened at Boulogne I noticed that one of the boxes was damaged at the sides. There was a hole that I could have put my finger in.'[45]

All this evidence from those employed at Folkestone and from the steamboat's mate made it clear to the jury that once the safes had arrived in Folkestone they were unloaded from the train, stored overnight and put on board the boat for Boulogne without any interference. Neither had they been tampered with in any way during the voyage.

The story then switched to the French side of the Channel. Giving his evidence through an interpreter, Jacques Thoron, the customs employee at Boulogne, concurred with Golder's views on the poor condition of one of the boxes:

On the arrival of the Folkestone boat on the morning of the 16th May, 1855, I assisted to land the bullion boxes. I took one of the boxes out of the iron chest myself, and I noticed that it was open at the sides, so that I could have put in my finger. I noticed through the opening that there was a little bag moving about inside. The boxes were placed on the quay, and they were never out of my sight till they were taken to the railway.[46]

James Major, for the French railway, also gave his account: 'I took charge of the bullion boxes on their arrival. I saw them weighed at the Custom-house, and then I had them taken to my office, where they remained until they were taken to the railway. I weighed them myself before they went from my office.'[47] He was also able to tell the jury that he had seen one of the wooden boxes a few days later in Paris and that it was 'filled with small bags of lead shot'.[48] The testimonies from the French side of the Channel all pointed to the fact that the wooden boxes had been emptied of their valuables on the English side.

Mrs Harriet Hooker from Folkestone was able to officially identify Agar and Pierce as the men who took lodgings from her in May 1854:

I live at Folkestone, between the upper and lower stations. In the month of May a man who called himself Adams took lodgings at my house for himself and another man. Agar is the man who went by the name of Adams. I saw him at the Mansion-house, and recognized him. The man who was with him at my house is Pierce, whom I see now, and recognize in the dock.[49]

Thomas Ledger, the railway clerk at Folkestone told the court about his meetings with Agar: 'I remember seeing Agar at Folkestone several times during the year 1854. I have seen him at the Rose inn ... and on one occasion he supped with myself and another person there. I saw him at Folkestone in the spring and in the autumn.'[50] When asked about the keys to the safes, he said: 'I had a key of the bullion chest, which I sometimes kept in my desk or in a cupboard which was behind me as I sat at my desk, but generally in my pocket.'[51] As to the office being left unattended when Agar claimed that he and Pierce had slipped in and made the wax impression of the key: 'I generally used to go down to meet the boats when they came in, but I left other persons in the office. Sometimes, however, I have known the office to be left empty – perhaps a dozen times.'[52]

Charles Chapman, the railway clerk, confirmed that Agar was in Folkestone in the spring and autumn of 1854. He told the court about Agar receiving a parcel through his office:

He came to me and inquired whether a parcel had arrived for him. Shortly afterwards a parcel did ... and I gave it to him out of the iron safe when he came for it. He signed a receipt for it in the waybill, for he said he could not write a receipt in full, as his finger was wounded. He had it bound up in a black silk stall.[53]

Chapman had to admit that it was possible that Agar could have seen where the key to the bullion safes was kept: 'If he had chosen, he could see where I took the key of the safe from.'[54]

After Chapman's examination concluded, the court was adjourned until 10 a.m. the following morning and the jury were brought 'to the London Coffee-house under the charge of the proper officers of the court'.[55]

CHAPTER 20

Day Two

---•---

The next morning, 14 January 1857, the trial at the Old Bailey resumed at the allotted time of 10 a.m. The first witness called was Charlemagne Everard, the assistant at Packham Neuffer & Co. in Paris. Like Jacques Thoron, he gave his evidence through an interpreter. He told the court about opening a delivery from Messrs Abel & Co. and finding only lead shot inside instead of gold bars. Thomas Sharman, the railway clerk, then gave his account of the activities of Agar and Tester at Folkestone. He told of how he went to the Royal Pavilion Hotel with Agar and Tester along with his friend, Greenstead.[1] He admitted that Inspector Hazel of the railway police had warned him about Agar, and that he had told Hazel he thought Agar was 'respectable' and that the inspector must have been 'misinformed' about him.[2]

Inspector Hazel was the next witness called to give evidence. He told the court that he had seen Pierce and Agar hanging around Folkestone and was suspicious of them. He also testified that he saw Agar with Tester:

I saw Pierce and Agar at Folkestone harbour in May, 1854. They were looking at the boat which ran in connection with the tidal train. They remained at the pier about a quarter of an hour, and then went away towards the town ... In October, 1854, I saw Agar loitering about the booking-office for about 10 minutes. He was watching the proceedings of the clerk,

Sharman, who was making up his money. I saw Agar talking to Tester by the pier on the following day. The boat was then getting ready. They afterwards walked towards the Pavilion Hotel. Tester went up to London the same night.[3]

Hazel said that he warned Sharman about Agar because he did not like the 'appearance' of the man. He was also suspicious about Tester, but he did not mention this to Sharman as he 'seemed to know him well'.[4] Hazel told the court how he had passed his suspicions on to Superintendent Steer of Folkestone Police. Controversially, he also commented on how, after the robbery, he was told to keep quiet about what he knew: 'I did not at first tell all I knew, because I was told by the police that it might frustrate the ends of justice if I did so. Captain Barlow, the manager of the company, gave me the same directions.'[5] Superintendent Steer also gave evidence. He stated that after he was told about these two men, he saw them himself:

I was at Folkestone in May, 1854. I saw Pierce half-way between that town and Hythe, in company with a man named Adams … They were at Folkestone in the spring for about a fortnight, and walked a good deal on the pier. When they saw that I observed them they separated and walked away. In October I again saw Agar, near the Pavilion Hotel.[6]

His testimony linked Burgess with Agar because he said that he saw them together 'on one occasion … near Folkestone harbour'.[7]

The two members of staff from Dover station – Henry Williams, the booking clerk, and Joseph Witherden, the porter – were called to give their accounts of the suspicious men who had passed through their station on the night of the robbery. Williams remembered the details of the night well:

I attended the departure of the 2am up train … [and] saw two passengers who travelled first-class by it. They carried bags with them. I noticed them pass through the office while Burgess,

Kennedy, and I were standing there together. A porter asked to carry their bags for them. One of the two men was taller than the other; the one was of light complexion and the other dark. I issued two tickets only for that train, but not to the two passengers I have described, who did not apply for any tickets.[8]

There had been laughter in court earlier when Agar had explained that Witherden had asked no more questions about their trip from Ostend, or their unusual dearth of luggage, when some silver was placed in his palm. Witherden was now called on to give his account of their exchange that night:

... two men, carrying carpet-bags, and wearing short cloaks, came on to the platform without taking tickets. The bags they had appeared to be heavy, from the way in which they carried them. [I] Spoke to them about their tickets. They produced two Ostend return tickets. I asked whether their luggage had passed the Customs House. They replied, 'No; it came over the previous night.' One of them gave me some money; I don't know which of the two it was.[9]

Mr Werter Clark, the owner of the Rose Inn in Dover, told the court about two men – one 'tall and dark', the other 'short and fair' – who stayed at his establishment around the time in question, and how they had asked for directions to Folkestone. 'I directed them,' he said, 'to the road thither by the cliffs.'[10] Robert Clark, the waiter at the Dover Castle Hotel, also gave evidence regarding two men with remarkably similar descriptions to those already mentioned. He said that he served these men one night around the time that the robbery was committed and they told him that they were travelling up to London by the 2 a.m. train:

One of them was considerably shorter than the other. The complexion of the short man was fair; the tall one was dark. They asked for some brandy and water; which they wished to be put into a sodawater bottle. I got it for them. They left the hotel later the same night, carrying their own luggage. They said they were going by the 2am train.[11]

The jury listened to Matthew Dickenson, the porter at London Bridge station, as he spoke of the two men who disembarked from the Dover to London train on the morning of 16 May and how one, at least, was carrying a bag:

> I recollect the 2 a.m. train arriving from Dover on the morning of the 16th of May, 1855, about 4 o'clock; only about four passengers came by it. Two men came out of a carriage that I opened. One of them was taller and of darker complexion than the other. The man who first left the carriage had a bag with him, and wore a loose cape. I did not notice the dress of the other man. I offered to get a cab for them. They declined my offer....'[12]

His fellow porter, William Woodhouse, testified that the luggage van had no luggage on board that morning. He said that he also saw the two men, but only at some distance away from him on the platform, and he would not be able to recognize them again.

Stephen Jones, the guard with the South Eastern Railway, told the jury about being on the earlier 7.30 p.m. train from Dover one evening in May 1855, and arriving at Reigate station around 9.25 p.m. He saw Tester come out of the refreshment room and board a First Class carriage. Tester was carrying 'a black leather bag of 12 to 15 inches in length'.[13] Jones was only on that train that particular night, he said, because he had been assigned to the same train for both April and May. (This, of course, was because of Tester's alteration of the guards' work roster.) Jones had passed this off as nothing unusual when he first spoke at the Mansion House, until he was contradicted by his colleague, John Peake Knight. By this time his opinion was that to be assigned to work on the same train for more than a month could happen, but was unusual: '... it is usual for the guards to be one month on a train – it sometimes happens they are more – it has happened about three times to my knowledge ... I have been on one train for many months, but that is a special service....'[14] Jones also testified that he saw Pierce and Burgess, both of whom he knew, together in London in 1853 at the Green Man public house in Tooley Street. He also said that he had seen Pierce in Folkestone in 1854 in the company of some man whom he did not know. He saw the two of them together on the pier at Folkestone four or five times. He had not seen Pierce since. Jones said that he first heard of the robbery five or six days after it happened, but he only mentioned Tester and the black bag a month or five weeks before the trial. He only mentioned it then, he said, because he had heard about Agar's evidence: 'I read a portion of Agar's evidence ... in which he charged Tester with being an accomplice....'[15] He explained how the investigators had never asked him anything about Tester. He had been asked about Pierce, he said, but never about Tester.

Frederick Russell, the booking clerk at London Bridge station, told the story of Tester coming into his office that evening in May after ten o'clock. Tester told him that 'he had come up from Reigate by the Dover line....'[16] Russell recalled that Tester had 'a black leather bag with him' that evening. It 'looked new', he said, and was 'about 15 inches long'.[17] Tester put the bag down in the booking-office and went out of the office for a while. Russell remembered the night-watchman, John Perry, coming in, lifting it up and remarking upon how heavy it was. Russell and Tester travelled home together that night on the Greenwich train, which was not, according to Russell, Tester's usual routine. Perry testified that he had lifted Tester's bag that night and it was 'heavy and "lumpy", just as though a stone was in it'.[18]

Mr John Chubb, 'the eminent locksmith', testified that his company had been requested to 'make several alterations' to the number one locks on each of the safes they had supplied to the South Eastern Railway.[19] He explained: 'The orders for these alterations were given by letters written in the handwriting of

Tester, and signed by [the superintendent] Mr Brown.'[20] This work, he said, necessitated the sending of keys to the superintendent's office.[21] Chubb revealed his shock in finding out, after the robbery had taken place, that the railway workers had not been using lock number two on any of the safes. These locks had become so corroded the keys would not move them anymore. It was clear to him that they had been that way for some considerable time.

John Peake Knight told the court that, at the time of the robbery, he was a superintendent at London Bridge station. He gave evidence regarding Tester's altering of the guards' roster and also about a conversation that took place, shortly after he joined the railway company, between Brown and Tester regarding the keys to the safes. To the best of his recollection that conversation concerned a key that had been lost by one of the captains of the steamboat. He remembered Tester being sent to Folkestone about it. He confirmed that, a few weeks later, several keys were sent to the office from the locksmith's. Knight testified that Brown usually took charge of the keys and that Tester's office was next to Brown's and opened onto it.

John Matthews, the manager of Messrs Massey money-changers in Leadenhall Street, and Rudolf Prommell, a Haymarket money-changer, were the first to give evidence about the disposal of the proceeds from the train robbery. Others would follow later. They told the court how they had bought American coin from a man on the morning of 16 May 1855, for £210 and £203 respectively. In Matthews' case the tall, tired man he remembered from that day resembled Pierce. Alexander White, the manager of the Charing Cross, Pall Mall East branch of the Union Bank of London, then confirmed that he cashed the cheque that Pierce had received from Prommell for sovereigns.[22]

Mary Ann Porter told of the Mr and Mrs Adams who had rented lodgings from her and her husband at 13 Harleyford Road, Vauxhall, in October 1854 and of their friend, whom she knew as Mr Peckham. She identified Agar as Mr Adams. Mr Adams and the woman described as his wife lodged there for about seven weeks, she said, and moved out a week before Christmas.[23] John Honnor of Walnut Tree Walk, Lambeth, described the 'nearly black' wig that he had 'dressed' for Pierce, who had been his neighbour and acquaintance of four or five years.

Before calling Fanny Kay to the stand it was decided to adjourn the trial for a short period in order to facilitate the taking of refreshment. Fanny's appearance at the trial was awaited with great anticipation.

CHAPTER 21

Intimately Acquainted

———•———

Fanny Kay was deemed to be so valuable a witness – and perhaps in sufficient danger – to be granted special protection prior to the trial. There may have been a fear that Pierce would arrange for someone to threaten her – or worse. In the weeks leading up to the trial, therefore, she was brought to live at Inspector Thornton's house, with all expenses paid for by the South Eastern Railway. She did not, however, seem very grateful for the company's hospitality: '... they do not allow me anything,' she complained. She said that they gave her food and lodging alright, but not clothes or money. Meanwhile, the great numbers of people who had been reading about the case in the newspapers were, understandably, anxious to see Fanny and hear what she had to say.

From the witness-box, just as she had at the Mansion House, the twenty-five-year-old Fanny spoke openly and unashamedly about her relationship with Agar: 'I was first introduced to Agar in 1853 by the prisoner Burgess. Some time after that introduction I became intimately acquainted with Agar, and had a child by him. In December, 1854, I went to live with him at Cambridge Villas, Shepherd's bush.'[1] She also told of her man's friendship with Pierce, who she said usually went under the name of Peckham. She described the activities that had been going on in their house around the time of the robbery: there were the many unexplained 'comings' and 'goings' with bags of various sizes; the activity in the wash-house; the night that Agar stayed out until the following morning. Then she told how, after that night away from home, Agar and Pierce brought some bags into the house and began to engage in more strange activities:

> ... after this time Pierce used to come very frequently to our house, and Agar and he were in an up-stairs room together for a long time each day, and I noticed that there was a very fierce fire. They were also in the wash-house together, and I often heard them hammering there. I only peeped once into the up-stairs room, and I then saw there was a large fire, and I often heard the fire roaring. On some occasions I also saw Pierce bring down what appeared to be pieces of stone; and when they came to their meals they were very hot and dirty.[2]

Fanny claimed that she never realized they were melting gold in the bedroom: '... I asked what they were doing, and they told me they were "leather apron weaving". After the noise had ceased I went into the room, and saw that the grate had been replaced, and that the floor of the room appeared to have been burned.'[3] She explained that Agar had left her shortly before he was arrested and convicted on the forgery charge. Nevertheless, she said, it was his wish that she and the child would be adequately provided for, and Pierce was supposed to take care of that. Agar had arranged for Pierce to have a more than sufficient amount of funds to do so; not only had he control of Agar's money, he had the remaining gold from the robbery and many of Agar's possessions at his house. She also claimed that in the past Agar had frequently helped Pierce by lending him money. Pierce, however, had refused to give her what she had been promised by Agar, and as a result she had gone to the authorities with her information about the train robbery.

The defence tried to discredit Fanny's testimony by asking questions about men with whom she might have had relationships, and suggesting that she had accepted money from them. She was adamant that she had not lived with any other man apart from Agar. She admitted to knowing an elderly man called

Tress, but said that she did not engage in any improper conduct with him. Mr Tress, she said, gave her money only once, £5, after she was dismissed from her job at Tunbridge station. She got to know a Mr Hart around six months after she left Tunbridge, but she did not live with him, nor was she 'in his company'.[4] Hart, who she said was thirty-five years of age at the time she knew him, came up to town once every two or three weeks, but did not stay with her. She admitted that he did give her a sovereign or two, 'but for no improper purpose'.[5] He used to call and see her after she left Tunbridge station, while she was living with her mother in London. He did not give her any money until after her mother had died. He did, however, make honourable proposals towards her.[6] The name of Bill Barber was also put to her, but she said that she did not keep company with him. He never gave her any money and, in fact, she did not even know if he was dead or alive. She admitted to knowing a man called Hodges, but said that he had never visited her: 'I have been in his company, but not for a very long time – he used to give me money, not less than a sovereign at a time.'[7]

Fanny was then questioned about her dismissal from her job at Tunbridge station. She was adamant that she was not dismissed for anything to do with dishonesty. In fact, she now claimed that she did not know why her employers had dismissed her: 'I do not know what they dismissed me for at Tunbridge – I do not know what complaint it was; I had done no harm – I had a very comfortable situation there, £12 a year and my board and lodging – I was not dismissed on account of improprieties with men....'[8]

On her relationship with Agar she revealed to the court that for a long time, until some time in 1854, she did not even know his real name: up until then she only knew him as 'Adams'. By the time their child was born she did know his real name and she said that the child was registered under that name.[9]

When questioned on her excessive drinking habits, Fanny denied that they were as bad as the prosecution were suggesting. While she was at Pierce's, she said, she was 'out all night for two nights ... not three nights'. She caused great hilarity in court when she was pushed further on the issue of her drinking and one incident in particular:

Q: Will you swear that you were never taken home drunk to Pierce's?

Fanny: No, I will not swear it, but I don't remember it.

Q: When you were living at Shepherd's bush, were you ever taken home in a wheelbarrow?

Fanny (Smiling at this): If I was, I don't recollect it.

Q: Might it have happened?

Fanny: Yes – once.

Q: More than once?

Fanny: No, I will swear that it might not have happened more than once.[10]

She admitted that Agar did leave her on two occasions but denied that on either occasion it was on account of her drinking '... he did not allege that as the reason that he left me, I was not in the habit of getting tipsy.'[11]

It was put to Fanny that the row with Pierce was also caused by her 'drunken habits'. Fanny was adamant that this was not the case. She denied that Mrs Pierce had complained frequently about her drinking, although she did admit to having an amicable chat with her about it: '... she has told me that it was a pity that I should do so, but merely in a friendly way; she never had occasion to complain of me in her house.'[12] Her falling out with Pierce was, she said, purely about the money that she had been promised by Agar. She said that Agar had told her, in a letter sent from prison, about the £3,000 that he had arranged to be given to Pierce in order to provide for her and the child. In the same letter he told her to buy the children – their boy and the Pierces' boy – 'two silver cups, and several other things'.[13] Fanny said that she discussed the contents of that letter with Mr and Mrs Pierce: 'Agar said that Pierce was to give me the money, and I told Pierce so, and his wife too.'[14] But Pierce's response was far from satisfactory: 'Pierce said that Agar never had any money, that he was mad ... Pierce told me he had no money....'[15] Fanny said that as a result of this they had an argument and she left their house. What Pierce gave her while Agar was in prison, she claimed, did not amount to £100 in total.[16] Regarding this money that Agar had promised her, she said that she had 'never heard anything of it since'.[17]

As Fanny's evidence came to a close, Mr Baron Martin interjected, saying that he wanted to get the facts about this money: '... consols to the amount of 3,000*l.* were transferred by Agar to some one for the use of this woman, and ... she has never seen the money. I should like to hear something about it.'[18]

As a result, Mr Wontner, who was acting as Pierce's solicitor at the trial but who had also handled this transaction for Agar, gave an account of the money. He was asked about the veracity of Fanny's claims, and his comments supported her contention firmly and categorically:

> Previous to Agar's conviction he had 3,000*l.* consols, which had been standing in his name for a long time, and he authorised a stockbroker to sell it out. That was done accordingly and the amount realized was about 2,700*l.* A number of payments were made out of that sum by Agar's authority, and he directed me to hand over the balance – 2,500*l.* – to Pierce to invest for Kay and her child (as we understood). He gave me a written order to that effect, and that order I executed.[19]

It was clear from Wontner's comments that, just as Fanny had claimed, Pierce was in control of Agar's funds and he was supposed to arrange for the financial support of Fanny and the child. He did invest the money in Turkish bonds, but then refused to give financial support to Fanny. When Fanny had finished giving her evidence there could be little doubt left in the mind of anyone present that Agar's wish regarding his money had been denied by Pierce, and the trust he had placed in Pierce had been mistaken.

Charlotte Paynter gave somewhat more detail in her testimony at the Old Bailey than she had done at the Mansion House. The fifteen-year-old servant from 8 Southampton Street, Vauxhall, told the court that she had been in the service of Mr and Mrs Adams at Harleyford Road for two or three months. She only ever knew Agar as Mr Adams. Her main job, she explained, was to mind the child. She told of how she saw Pierce a number of times at Harleyford Road, and how he had assisted them when they relocated to Cambridge Villas in very cold weather around Christmas time. She thought then that his name was 'Mr Peckham'. She remembered that he came to Cambridge Villas even more often than he had come to the other place. At the new premises she slept in the back room upstairs where there was a common stove, while Mr and Mrs Adams slept in the front room. She remembered that Pierce and Agar spent a lot of time together in the wash-house at the back of the house – sometimes all day. She never went in there while they were present and she could not see what was going on in there; nor did she hear anything. On one occasion when she tried to get in while they were there she found that the door was locked. She knocked, but her boss called out from inside that she could not come in. She did clean the wash-house when they were not present and she saw two boxes in there, a green one and a white one. The green box was produced in court and Charlotte identified it. She remembered having to push the boxes out of her way in order to sweep underneath them. 'They appeared to be heavy,' she said. She also remembered that there was a vice fixed in the wash-house. She also testified to seeing a drab bag on the premises. A leather bag was produced in court and she confirmed that it was like that one. She said that she once saw Agar come into the back parlour with that bag and put it on a chair.

Mary Ann Wilde, the servant to the Agars' next door neighbours at Cambridge Villas, Mr and Mrs Bessell, also gave evidence. She said that she slept in the back room upstairs of her house and from her bedroom window she could see the window of Mr Adams' wash-house. She identified Agar as the man she knew as Mr Adams. She saw him going into the wash-house with another man and heard frequent hammering from there. Just as he had at the Mansion House, Zaccheus Long confirmed that he rented his property at 4 Crown Terrace, Haverstock Hill, to Pierce from 18 December 1854 until 18 June 1855, at which stage Pierce moved out and went to next door. The owner of 3 Crown Terrace, John Carter, testified that Pierce moved into his premises in June 1855; but only stayed for around a month.[20]

Next came the testimony of the cab drivers. William Ellis Wood, who lived at Hawley Mews, Hawley Street, Camden Town, told the court that he drove one of his own cabs, no. 3016. He testified that in the spring of 1855 he was hailed by a man around seven or half past seven in the evening. He took this man to somewhere near the Prince of Wales Road, stopping about two or three hundred yards from Crown Terrace, at the corner of the main road. The man asked him to wait there as he went off towards Crown Terrace. The man returned with another man, who was four or five inches taller. He remembered that these men were carrying two or three bags: one leather bag, he thought, and two carpet-bags. As he did not lift them himself, he could not say if these bags were heavy or light. Both men seemed to be carrying mantles or cloaks over their arms, which he thought they put on when they got out of the cab later. He was taking them, as instructed, to London Bridge station, but when they got over London Bridge they told him to stop by the London Bridge Hotel. One of the men then got out and walked in the direction of either London Bridge station or Tooley Street. The other man remained in the cab and ordered Wood to drive on to St Thomas Street. When they got there, the man had him stop outside Guy's Hospital. The man who had got out of the cab earlier arrived about a quarter of an hour later. The men then ordered Wood to take them back to where they had come from. When he got to Hampstead Road, they ordered him to go instead to the Mother Shipton public house, located some two or three hundred yards from Crown Terrace, where they discharged him and went off with their bags.

About a week later, or perhaps less, Wood was again hailed off the rank near Chalk Farm by the smaller man. Again they proceeded to pick up another taller man. He was sure that the smaller man was the same, but he could not be sure about the taller one. They carried the same bags, though. He drove them to St Thomas Street where the shorter man got out. Wood thought that he was away for about a half or three quarters of an hour. When he came back, Wood took them once again to about two hundred yards from Crown Terrace, and they walked off with their luggage. Wood testified that he carried the two men again, for a third time, maybe a week later, and everything happened the same way. It was the shorter man who always gave the directions about where to go and Wood got the impression that he might be a valet to the taller man.

The other cab driver, Joseph Carter of Camden Town, gave his account of a similar experience, although it only happened to him on one occasion. He was hired by the two men in Camden Town, at least eighteen months previous to the trial. He knew these two men, having seen them before around the area, and unlike Wood was able to tell the court definitively that 'Pierce was one of the men, and Agar the other'.[21] Carter was on the rank in Camden High Street, probably around five or six o'clock – not as late as nine o'clock, anyway – when the two men came along carrying two if not three bags. By the way they put them into his cab, Carter judged their bags to be heavy. He brought them to St Thomas Street, stopping on the left-hand side at the bottom. Then Agar got out of the cab while Pierce remained inside. Carter told the court that he believed that Agar walked in the direction of London Bridge station. He came back half an hour later and Carter heard him say to Pierce, 'It is not going down tonight'.[22] Carter then drove them to the Mother Shipton public house where they got out and took their bags. As he drove away, Carter said he looked back and saw them both going along Prince's Terrace towards Crown Terrace.

Following the evidence given by the cab drivers, John Peake Knight was re-examined and was able to give some extra information about the geography of the area around London Bridge station: 'I have been at the place which the cabmen have described, near St. Thomas's Hospital – there are two ways from that place up to the station – there are two sets of steps; one leads from Joiner Street up to the Brighton station, and the other from Tooley Street up to the Greenwich side of the station.'[23]

In May, June and July 1855, James Clements kept a coffee-shop in Camden High Street, adjoining the Southampton Arms near the turnpike. In his evidence he said that he remembered two men of the same description as that given by the cab drivers, one shorter in height than the other, coming into his premises one evening 'about the middle of May'.[24] He noticed at least one carpet-bag in their possession. One of the men went away for about an hour and when he came back they both left. He did not see if they took a cab and he never saw them again.

John Allday, the boy who lived at Newbury Mews, Haverstock Hill, not far from Crown Terrace, testified that he and a number of his friends had found some lead shot lying around the area known as Prince's Terrace. He said that 'it was strewn along the road by the side of the kerb'.[25] They picked up handfuls of it. It was in two or three sizes. He was shown some of the lead shot used in the robbery and he said that some of it was the same size and some 'a little larger'.[26]

In order to corroborate the claim that Agar, Pierce, Tester and Burgess knew each other well and had worked together as accomplices, a number of innkeepers and their employees were brought in to testify to the fact that the gang members were often seen together in their establishments. One of these was Emma May, who had already spoken at the Mansion House. She testified that she worked for five and a half years as a servant to Mrs Thomas who kept the Marquis of Granby public house at New Cross. She was, she said, very familiar with Burgess, Pierce and Agar, although she did not know their names until recently. Burgess, she said, '... was in the habit of coming to the Marquis of Granby – he lived near there'.[27] She also knew Pierce and said that he, too, frequented the Marquis of Granby. 'They used to come in the morning between 11 and 12 o'clock,' she said, 'and in the evening between 7 and 8 o'clock.'[28] She also saw Agar there as often as the others. She testified to the fact that she saw them all together 'a good many times'.[29] According to her, they used to have a glass of beer or something to drink, but always drank moderately.

Walter Stearn of the White Hart public house in St Thomas Street, testified that he had known Pierce and Burgess for seven or eight years. They used to frequent his establishment both separately and together. He had also seen Agar there many times up until the middle of May 1855. He saw Agar with Burgess, two or three times, taking refreshment. Stearn also told his story about Burgess and his transaction with a large sum of money in February 1856. He told the court that in that month a parcel had been given to him by his servant. It was addressed to Burgess, who came in to collect it a day or two later. He opened it in front of Stearn and it contained notes to the value of around £500. Stearn said that Burgess asked his advice about what he should do with it. Stearn told him that he could deposit it in a bank. Stearn told him that, if he wished, he could bring it up to his brewers, Messrs Reid & Co., because they took money on deposit. Burgess agreed to this and Stearn took the money to Reid's and gave it to their cashier, John Smith. Afterwards Stearn received the interest due on the money, and left it with his barmaid for Burgess to collect. The book was produced in court, showing the entry on 19 February, the day on which the money was deposited by Stearn.

John Smith was also called to testify. He was able to confirm that on 19 February he received that deposit from Stearn. Smith had written on a number of the notes, and these were also produced as evidence in court. There were two £100 notes, five £50 notes, two £20 notes and one £10 note. They all had the name 'Stearn' clearly written on them in handwriting that Smith confirmed to be his own.

Sarah Thompson, Stearn's barmaid, testified that she, too, remembered the incident concerning the parcel of money for

Burgess. As far as she could remember, she had received the parcel from a person named Mr Lee.[30] She gave Stearn the parcel in February last, and only later found out that it contained money. She also remembered giving Burgess the £8 1s 1d that he had earned in interest, and showing him the account book as she did so.

Richard Lee, a stockjobber based at Charlotte Street, Camberwell, gave evidence that elucidated the story behind this parcel of money that had arrived at the White Hart for Burgess. He had worked formerly as a clerk for the South Eastern Railway on the old Croydon line and so he had known Burgess for eight or nine years and Tester for perhaps four years. He said that he also knew Pierce from his time as an employee with the railway. Lee frequented Stearn's public house and he saw Burgess there occasionally. At the beginning of February 1856, Lee met Burgess at Stearn's and Burgess asked him for some professional advice. He wanted to know if Lee could give him any information about purchasing Turkish bonds. Lee told him that he could, and Burgess asked him their price. Lee referred to the newspaper and found out that they were valued at around £8 at the time. After a discussion, Burgess gave him instructions to buy around £500 worth. Lee was quite happy to go ahead, feeling as he did that Burgess had 'always borne the character of an honest man'.[31] He went to Hutchinson's, the brokers, and bought the stock through them for £407 10s. Lee then brought the note of purchase to Burgess at Stearn's. Lee went to New Cross a day or two later and got the money from Mrs Burgess, as had been arranged with Burgess. She gave him £405 in notes and £2 10s in gold. He paid the same notes over to Hutchinson. He wrote down the numbers of them on a piece of paper and left this at New Cross in Mrs Burgess's safe keeping. He also wrote his name on the notes. Three £100 notes and eight £10 notes were produced as evidence in court, and Lee testified that the writing on them was his own. He said that five weeks later he sold the Turkish bonds for £464 7s 6d, again through Hutchinson's. He received a cheque for them on 15 February, a cheque he had cashed. Having taken his commission, he put Burgess's money, in notes, into an envelope, and this was the parcel that he gave to Miss Thompson at Stearn's for Burgess to collect.

In other attempts to trace the money trail generated by the illicit proceeds from the train robbery, a number of witnesses were called to give evidence regarding financial transactions. Richard Adye Bailey, a clerk in the banknote office of the Bank of England, was one of these. He gave evidence regarding the six £100 notes that had been paid out of his bank in the name of Edgington on 28 May 1855. It was supposed that the name of Edgington had been used by the robbers because Edgington's were a company of 'large tarpaulin manufacturers in the neighbourhood of the station' and were 'familiar to the servants of the South Eastern Railway Company'.[32] It was clear now that the transaction was fraudulent and had nothing to do with Edgington's. These notes were important because there was evidence to indicate that they had been in the hands of the defendants. In fact, they were some of the notes that had been given out by Pierce when the first tranche of the spoils from the robbery was being divided up. The bank books were produced as evidence in court and, as a number of the actual notes had come back into the bank, they were produced as well. They were numbered from 45420 to 45425.[33]

Three of the notes could be traced back through the stockbrokers Curtis & Co. and Hutchinson & Co. to Lee and ultimately back to the purchase of those Turkish bonds for Burgess. The note numbered 45420 was returned to the bank on 14 Sepember 1855 with the name of Tester written on it, but with the Christian name torn off. The note numbered 45422 came in on 11 September 1855 and had written on it 'Wm. Geo. Tester, 11 Sep., 6 St. Jermyn's Villas, Lewisham'. John Peake Knight was called to the stand once again to verify whether the names on the notes were, in fact, in Tester's own handwriting, to which he said: 'I know the writing very well from his being in the same office with me. And I saw his writing daily – there is no concealment about it; it is quite the style.'[34]

One of the £100 notes, number 44525, paid in on 21 November 1855, had 'Geo. Raffan, 72 Warren Street, Fitzroy Square' written on it, as well as 'Henry Fisher' and 'R.B.', for Royal British.[35] In order to elucidate the story of this note, George Raffan was called as a witness. He said that he had been employed by Pierce from the beginning of 1855 into 'a portion' of 1856, a period of somewhat less than two years. He resigned from the position in the June or July prior to the trial. Raffan told the court that he had received thirty shillings a week in wages. He also testified that Pierce kept a betting house: 'I know that Pierce had a book of more than 100*l*. on the St. Leger the year Saucebox won.'[36] Raffan said that he frequently, as part of his job, went to get notes changed for Pierce: '... I have been in the habit of changing notes for him frequently ... notes taken in business from the gentlemen with whom he bet ... I have known considerable sums of money in his possession from time to time arising from betting transactions.'[37] As for the £100 note numbered 44525, Raffan explained how, about twelve or thirteen months before the trial, Pierce had asked him to get change for a £100 Bank of England note. Raffan remembered that he wrote his name on the note and took it to a Mr Fisher in Cranbrook Street to exchange for smaller notes. The note numbered 44525, Raffan said, was the note in question and he identified his writing on it. He said that, perhaps a month later, Pierce sent him to the Bank of England with an amount of notes for which he received two hundred sovereigns. He remembered the precise instructions given to him by Pierce on that occasion: '... he told me to go over to the far end and I should see a little desk, and I could write my name on one of them – I did so, and got the money in gold for the notes.'[38]

In the end, all of this seemed to lead to the conclusion expressed by Shee: 'There can be no doubt, therefore, I submit to you, that the prisoners shared that £600.'

An array of bankers, clerks and stockbrokers were brought into court to prove that, following the train robbery, the three defendants were in possession of a greater amount of money than their positions of employment could possibly explain: Alfred Joseph Young, a stock and share broker; William Sinclair St George Forrester, a stockbroker based at Angel Court, Throgmorton Street; Benjamin Page, who was related to Tester by marriage and was the holder of a bond that was the property of Tester but which, according to Page, was given to him by Tester's father; William Cock Tilley and Archibald Griffiths, both clerks with the Bank of England; Edward Natali Francis, the partner from the firm of Edgington & Co. of Duke Street; and Charles Cousins, clerk to Messrs Hutchinson & Co., the Lothbury stockbrokers.[39] The money trail exposed a complicated story of changing cash, purchasing bonds, dates, serial numbers, names written on notes, and so on. In the end even the judge, Mr Baron Martin, failed to see where all this financial evidence was leading, and he ruled that it not be pursued any further.[40]

John Rees was the next witness to take the stand. He told the court that on the day that Pierce was arrested he went to search Pierce's lodgings at Kilburn Villa. He explained what he saw in the pantry at the basement level of the house:

> I found that the ground had been disturbed ... a hole had evidently been dug there at some former time, and in place of the clay which was the natural formation of the ground ... the hole was filled with loose cinders and rubbish, there were appearances which enabled me to judge how recently the hole had been filled up, in the cinders were fresh leaves and autumn berries, and part of the claw of a lobster, evidently quite fresh....[41]

His inference was that this had been the hiding-place for the gold, which by the time he got there had been moved. He explained to the court that hidden in various places throughout the house were Turkish bonds to the value of £2,600, deeds, leases, securities, IOUs and promissory notes. He also found the green tool-box in the attic.[42] Rees also told of his discoveries at

Agar's former address of 3 Cambridge Villas. These, he testified, included evidence of a very hot fire:

> I found an ordinary stove in the chimney place – I caused it to be removed ... the chimney was entirely free from soot, and had evidently been subjected to a very intense heat – I examined the bricks and found appearances of gold on them – I looked at the floor – I found the boards had been burnt in several places – I caused some of the boards to be taken up where the burning was, and I found several small particles of gold – they had evidently dropped through the boards onto the ceiling below....

When called on to testify, Inspector Williamson told how he had accompanied Rees to the house in Kilburn Villa. Along with the items already listed by Rees he mentioned their discovery of the gold watch and chain and at least one betting book.

Williamson was the final witness called in this intriguing trial. Those on the prosecution side now hoped that they had managed to build up a compelling case to prove that the three defendants, Pierce, Burgess and Tester, along with the witness, Agar, had worked together to plan and commit the Great Train Robbery of 1855.

But then, before the trial finished for the second day, there was another sensational turn of events. Parry announced that he wished to raise an important point of law on behalf of his client, Pierce.[43] With the judges' permission, Parry proceeded to object to three of the indictments as far as they were being applied to his client. He said that Pierce could perhaps be called to answer on the count of simple larceny but not on the other three counts, which related to stealing from his masters, stealing the property in the dwelling house of the company and feloniously receiving the stolen goods. Unlike Burgess and Tester, he argued, his client was not an employee of the railway company at the time of the alleged robbery; therefore, even if he was involved, he could not be indicted for stealing from his masters. Also, the charge of larceny in a dwelling house 'could not be supported' for any of the clients because 'a railway carriage could scarcely be called a dwelling house'. Finally, he said, contrary to Pierce being a receiver of stolen goods, 'the evidence pointed quite the other way'.

Parry's statement may have come as a surprise to many in court, yet there did appear to be some merit in his argument. This was made apparent to all when the judges found it necessary to confer with each other on the matter. After some minutes deliberation, and albeit reluctantly, Mr Baron Martin announced that he was forced to accept Parry's argument: '... it was clearly disproved that Pierce was a servant of the company at the time of the robbery. On that count of the indictment there was no evidence to go to the jury ... Pierce could not be called a receiver. As to the third count there would scarcely be any necessity to trouble the jury on that.'[44]

Amazingly, this development meant that Pierce could now only be judged, and if found guilty sentenced, on a charge of 'simple larceny'. This led to a scenario where Burgess and Tester would, if found guilty, be treated much more harshly than Pierce. Therefore, of the two career criminals and main instigators of the crime, one of them, Agar, was acting as a witness and would never stand trial for the crime, and the other, Pierce, would now receive a lighter sentence than the two men he had corrupted into taking part in the crime. With that shock to everyone's sense of justice, the court adjourned until ten o'clock the following morning, and the jury was once again sent to the London Coffee House to rest and contemplate the day's events.

CHAPTER 22

A Very Romantic Story

O n Thursday morning, 15 January 1857, the trial entered its final day. The excitement was palpable and the courtroom 'was filled, as on previous occasions, with an anxious and atten- tive audience'.[1] Throughout the trial, as details of the lifestyles being led by Agar and Pierce were revealed to the public, it is not surprising that there was a general sense of outrage. *The Times* reflected this feeling:

> … its most alarming feature is that men so determined and so skilful should be possessed of the means of subsistence for so long a time. Agar with his 3,000*l*., Pierce with his house at Kilburn, all of them driving about for a year in cabs, and jour- neying up and down the South Eastern line with first-class tickets, form a picture of criminal prosperity which we had hardly looked for.'[2]

As the proceedings of the final day got under way, Pierce's counsel, Parry, was given his last opportunity of addressing the jury and swaying the verdict in his client's favour. As the pris- oners themselves were precluded from giving evidence or addressing the jury, these final statements were of the utmost importance. Parry began by once again warning the jury members not to be influenced by any comments or reports that they may have seen in the press. If they had read any comments that would 'impair the impartiality with which they should view the case', he asked that they 'endeavour to let them pass away altogether from their recollection'.[3] He expressed his displeasure about some of the coverage that had been in the press: 'With a free press it was absolutely necessary that reports of proceedings in courts of justice should be made public, and he did not complain of that; but what he did complain of was that comments were made upon cases that were under discussion adverse to the parties accused....'[4] He asserted that 'there was not a tittle of actual evidence against any of the prisoners except the statement of their accomplice'. Therefore, he turned his attention to the credibility of that accomplice. He referred to the comments made by Shee at the opening of the trial regarding the fact that 'he did not ask them to convict ... unless the evidence of Agar, the accomplice, were confirmed and corroborated by other witnesses'.[5] But, argued Parry, according to 'the principles which the judges invariably laid down on such occasions ... an accomplice should be corroborated in his evidence, not merely as to the facts of the case ... but ... also in reference to the "person" of the accused ... and ... in all material and substantial particulars'.[6] This, he inferred, had not been achieved in the presentation of this case. Of course Agar knew the particulars of the crime – he was after all involved in it – but this did not prove that the defendants were involved. Parry argued that there had been no corroboration to prove that Pierce was involved in this crime. He warned the jury that 'when a man knew that he was charged with an offence ... he might endeavour to purchase immunity for himself by falsely accusing others'.[7] This, according to him, was what Agar was doing.

Parry quoted from judgements made by Lord Arbinger and Baron Alderson in similar cases. Arbinger said that 'corroboration ought to consist in some circumstance that affects the identity of the party accused. A man who has been guilty of a crime himself will always be able to relate the facts of the case, and ... that is really not corroboration at all.'[8] Alderson's judgement, meanwhile, required that juries always seek corroboration that 'goes to fix the guilt on the particular person charged'.[9]

Parry put it to the jury that in the case of his client, 'according to the law and the practice of the courts the evidence before them failed to substantiate his guilt'.[10]

Then Parry turned his attention to attacking Agar more directly, addressing the witness's character: '... it would be impossible ... to add to the detestation which they must all feel for the character of that man Agar. Rarely did they find ... such a man as Agar, having lived a course of crime and fraud of almost every description from the time that he was 18 or 20 years of age.'[11] Parry suggested to the jury that perhaps a deal had been done between Agar and the railway company for his eventual release:

> He wondered whether the influence of the South Eastern Railway Company would be sufficient to induce the Government to let loose a criminal like that again upon society. It was right that crime should be detected; but it was not right that men situated like Agar should be encouraged and invited, as he had been in this case, to make these revelations. He knew not whether we should have the happiness of claiming for ourselves the privilege of calling Mr Agar a free fellow-subject; he knew not whether he was again to be let loose upon the world; but evidently that was one of the motives which opened upon his mind; and the other a feeling of great malignity towards the prisoner Pierce.[12]

In the case of Agar he felt sure, he said, that the jury 'would know with what distrust to view the testimony of such a person....'[13]

As to the details of the evidence given, Parry admitted that Pierce knew Agar and that they had been seen together a number of times in Folkestone and elsewhere. But, he argued, none of that proved his client to have been involved in the robbery of the train:

> That Pierce and Agar were intimate there could be no question, but in what their intimacy consisted he knew not, and he did

not think that mere intimacy alone should weigh very strongly with the jury.[14]

There was no doubt that Agar committed the robbery, and if he wished to convict Pierce of the crime nothing was easier than for him to associate Pierce with himself upon that visit to Folkestone, although Pierce might have been perfectly innocent of any criminal intention.[15]

Yes, he conceded, there might be evidence to state that Agar went to Dover that night – but that had nothing to do with his client:

On the 15th May, 1855, Agar went down by mail train to Dover; but what he did while he was riding in the train, what he did at Dover, how he returned and with whom he returned, of his arrival in London and his return home, of the sale of the money by Pierce, and of every one of the circumstances which were really the leading circumstances of this robbery ... there was not a shadow of corroboration of the statement made by Agar. There was no proof that Pierce had been his companion upon that occasion or that he had had anything whatever to do with the matter.[16]

There was also no corroboration, said Parry, of Pierce's involvement in the 'long story told by Agar about obtaining possession of the key' or 'the purchase of the [lead] shot'. In addition, he argued that even if it were true, as Agar had alleged, that they had made a 'multiplicity of visits' to London Bridge station and St Thomas Street together, that did not prove that Pierce had done so with a view to committing a crime.[17]

He dismissed the evidence of Werter Clark and Robert Clark regarding the two men they had seen in Dover: '... they were seen by the two Clarkes [sic], the landlord and the waiter, in strong gaslight, and yet there was no identification of Pierce....'[18] Perhaps in a reference to his client's height, Parry commented that 'Pierce was by no means an ordinary looking man' and yet no one seemed to be able to positively identify him.[19] Also, he posed the question of why the railway staff did not recognize him:

> ... they passed through the station at 2 o'clock in the morning in such a manner as to attract the attention of three witnesses; they stayed 20 minutes on the platform; Agar said that he gave money there to a railway porter, and yet not one person identified Pierce ... Pierce, although he had been in the service of the railway company, and must have been known to many of the officers of the company, was not identified....[20]

He described as 'miraculous' this idea that Pierce, 'being known to the railway officers, should have passed them without being observed'.[21] He also rejected the idea of a disguise:

> Agar stated that Pierce had disguised himself with a wig and whiskers, and the only evidence in support of that statement was that a wig had been dressed for him in October, 1854.[22]
> ... There was no proof whatever that Pierce was disguised upon the night in question, for the logic of a person who would say that because a man had a wig dressed in October, 1854, therefore he was disguised in it in May, 1855, although it might suit the brain of Agar, was not logic ... which would impose upon the jury, or which would induce them to say that there was an atom of corroboration of the statement of Agar, that Pierce was a co-operator and participator with him in this particular act.[23]

Parry argued that although it was proved in court that some of the stolen gold was sold, it had not been proved that Pierce had anything to do with selling it. Neither could his client be linked in any way with the hiring of carts used 'to carry the booty', as Agar had claimed.[24]

Parry reminded the members of the jury that they were not

deciding the fate of his client on issues such as whether Pierce and Agar knew each other, or had spent time in each other's company, or had travelled in a cab together at some particular time. Their duty was, he told them, to determine '... what took place from half past 8 o'clock on the night of the 15th of May, 1855, when the Dover express started, until the time when it arrived in Dover'.[25] Their duty was 'to ascertain whether Pierce was the companion of Agar on that journey of plunder, which no doubt would become memorable in the annals of crime', but, he told them, 'there was not one tittle of corroboration in that respect'.[26]

Parry dealt with Fanny's evidence in a similarly dismissive manner: '... who was this Fanny Kay?' he wondered. Was she, he asked, 'a witness on whom they could rely?'[27] He urged the jury members to consider: 'had she not in all probability gone in there with a fixed resolution to make good her object of revenge against Pierce?'[28] He branded her as 'immoral'.[29] He went through, once again, the list of male acquaintances with whom she had been linked in court: Mr Hart, Mr Tress, Mr Barber. He emphasized how she and Agar had 'lived together as man and wife for two years'. He said that 'Serjeant Shee, with a face more innocent than his learned friend usually wore', had asked Fanny about these things. But Shee, he said, 'had the innocence, or assumed it, to re-examine her so as to induce them to believe that all her attachments were honourable'.[30] This, Parry insisted, was not the case. 'Not only was she profligate,' he said, 'but she was addicted to habits of intoxication,' which '... tended to weaken the intellect both of man and woman – it was one of the most degrading vices that either sex could be guilty of, and every one must admit that its effect was to blind the moral sense and to darken and to diminish the distinctions between right and wrong.'[31]

They all knew that Agar was a criminal, Parry claimed, and therefore he asked, 'could such a woman live with such a man and remain untainted? ... Could such a woman live with such a man, and remain a pure-minded and honourable woman?'

'Pure,' he asserted, 'she could not be.'[32] He had no doubt, he told the court, 'that she had coloured and exaggerated if ... not created the larger portion of her evidence'.[33] What Fanny wanted, according to Parry, was 'to convict and to punish, and to be revenged upon Pierce'. Therefore, he called on the jury members to 'reject the evidence of Fanny Kay as unworthy and unreliable, and to consider that Agar and Kay were really one and the same person in this trial, and that they were both actuated by the same motives'.[34]

On the question of the money trail that the prosecution had claimed was a product of the train robbery, Parry pointed to the fact that there was only one £100 note that the prosecution had managed to link with his client. This note was one of those given out by the Bank of England on 28 May 1855, in the name of Edgington, and was then changed by Raffan for Pierce in November of 1855. But, Parry argued, this was when Agar was under arrest, and 'he asked the jury how they could say that that was not one of the notes which Agar had left with Pierce to be applied to the support of Kay?'[35] Said Parry: 'No other proceeds of this robbery had been traced to Pierce, and if, as had been proved, Pierce had from time to time advanced to Fanny Kay from 80*l.* to 100*l.*, what more likely than that he should have changed the note in question to supply her with money?'[36] Parry's statement ended with the clear contention that his client was innocent and must, therefore, be acquitted.

Giffard, when he got his opportunity to speak on behalf of Burgess, also cast doubt on the reliability and trustworthiness of the principal witness. He said that Agar's '... character was so bad that it was impossible to blacken it ...' and that Agar 'was endeavouring to escape punishment or to avenge himself by the betrayal of his accomplices....'[37] There was no proof, he said, that Burgess was involved at all with this train robbery. Just because Agar knew the names of a few railway employees, that did not prove anything: 'It might be true that he had been meditating the crime for years and endeavouring to corrupt the railway servants, and that in the steady pursuit of that object he had scraped an acquaintance with some of them, and had been seen from time to time in their company....'[38] Giffard argued that Agar was just as likely to have accused Sharman or any other railway employee in the same way that he had done with Burgess. He asserted that there was no proof that the robbery had even taken place on Burgess's train: the gold, he claimed, could just as easily have been stolen while it was at the station or at the harbour at Folkestone. He suggested an alternative scenario: '... the key which the captain of the vessel had lost, Agar by some extraordinary coincidence had found. Agar being compelled to fix the scene of the robbery some-where fixed it in the train; but might it not have occurred just as easily ... at the station or on the quay waiting for the boat?'[39] Giffard also said that he could not see how Agar could have got out of the luggage-van at Dover without being seen: after all, '... there were porters always in attendance ... and if Agar had got out of the guards' van at the station would it not have created remark?'[40] In fact, he said, if you were to believe Agar, by the time they reached Dover there were three of them in the guard's van, as Pierce had joined them at Reigate. 'If three persons then got out of the van at the station,' he asked, 'must it not have led to inquiry, and would not the jury have expected some evidence on that subject?' He cast doubt on Agar's story of having travelled six or seven times on Burgess's train in order to test and refine the copied keys. According to him: '... he could scarcely get into the guard's van upon all those occasions without having been seen by some of the porters or the underguard.'[41]

Giffard criticized the evidence given by the underguard on the train that night, John Kennedy. In particular, he said, Kennedy's comments about not having seen anything of Burgess once he got on the train until they arrived in Dover 'left the impression that Burgess was working away in the van with Agar during the whole of the journey down'.[42]

It had not been proved, he said, that there was a close relationship between Agar and Burgess. Even Fanny Kay, he recounted, had admitted in her evidence that she had not seen Burgess once 'during the whole two years' that she had lived with Agar.[43] This, he said, could hardly 'be reconciled with the alleged fact that Burgess was concerned in the robbery'.[44]

As to the division of the spoils, Giffard had some difficulties with Agar's evidence there. He argued that it was hard to believe, as was claimed, that two of the alleged gang members had waited patiently for months to receive their share. This, he said, 'was not in accordance with human nature that a man who had run such risks for spoil should be so indifferent about getting his share of it....'[45] Then there was this assertion that they had accepted their payment from Pierce in notes. This he thought to be extremely improbable: 'Was it to be believed that persons trained in crime, who had got gold coin, which could not be traced, as the fruits of their robberies, would be likely to exchange it for bank notes, for tracing which there were such facilities?'[46] In any event, he believed that his client had nothing to answer with regard to these notes: 'It was not alleged that it was Burgess who obtained these notes at the bank, and little weight could therefore be attached to the circumstance of some of them coming into his possession eight or nine months afterwards.'[47] Yes, he admitted, there was evidence that his client had purchased a number of Turkish bonds, but this 'only proved that by a successful speculation he was able to clear the sum of £60. The guard of a train had many opportunities of knowing the state of the market, and, hearing that those bonds were "up" he might reasonably have thought it a good time for dealing in them.'[48] There was no proof, however, that any of this was a product of crime.

Giffard said that the allegation made by Agar that Burgess had signalled to him that the robbery was to go ahead on the 15 May 1855 by wiping his face went 'wholly uncorroborated'.[49] He also ridiculed the idea that Burgess, had he been involved in planning a robbery such as this, would have been foolish enough to meet with his accomplices at a busy place like the Marquis of Granby public house. He assured the jury that Agar's version of events was no more than an invention: '... Agar had, no doubt, told a very romantic story, and one that might very well be made the subject of a drama ... [but] there really was no material fact that in any way tended to show that Agar was speaking the truth when he alleged that the prisoner Burgess was concerned in the robbery.'[50]

Giffard complained about the behaviour of the South Eastern Railway Company in the aftermath of the robbery. He said that when Messrs Abel & Co. claimed compensation from the railway they were 'resisted ... from May to September on the grounds that the gold had been stolen in France'. Then they told Inspector Hazel 'to say nothing upon the subject of the robbery during the period when they were disputing their liability'.[51] The findings from the inquiry into the robbery, as a part of which Burgess was examined, were 'bottled up' by the company for eighteen months. This, he said, meant that so much time had passed when Burgess was finally apprehended that he had been 'most unfairly deprived of the legitimate means of making good his defence'.[52]

Giffard concluded his statement by reminding the members of the jury about Burgess's record of good character and his length of unblemished service with the South Eastern Railway Company. He asked them to contrast the reputation of Burgess with the word of Agar, a man 'steeped in crime from his earliest years'.[53] Giffard 'submitted that the case was not one free from all reasonable doubt; that Burgess was therefore entitled to the benefit of his previous good character; and he confidently believed that his client would meet with an acquittal.'[54]

After some refreshment, Ballantine was called on to make his final address to the jury on behalf of his client, Tester. He, too, began by asking the jury members 'to dismiss from their minds all that they had learnt of this from the newspapers and other extraneous sources'.[55] He told them that much of what had been introduced as evidence over the past few days had been 'invented and applied with an ingenuity perfectly devilish, but which the careful scrutiny of honest and unprejudiced minds would unravel and defeat'.[56] His client, he said, had held 'an onerous and well-remunerated situation' with the South Eastern Railway Company and was 'the son of a man of substance and respectability'.[57] When he left the company of his own accord, in 1856, Tester 'entered upon an office equally responsible and more lucrative in the service of a railway company in Sweden'.[58] Ballantine reminded the jury that Tester could have chosen to stay in Sweden instead of attending this trial: 'he ... preferred to place himself voluntarily within the reach of punishment, and now stood of his own accord in the felons' dock.'[59]

Again, like the counsels representing Pierce and Burgess, Ballantine claimed that Agar's evidence concerning his client was full of lies. Tester, according to him, was wholly innocent and had only been chosen by Agar in order to build up a convincing but false story about how the gold had been stolen. He gave his opinion of Agar to the court and held nothing back:

> ... a scoundrel, and a scoundrel of no ordinary stamp. As a psychological phenomenon his character deserved careful study ... the only part of his life of which he was ashamed and which he sought to hide was the three years of wasted honesty during which he held a humble situation, and did not sully his hands with renewed crime. His general career, marked by masterly contrivance and perverted forethought, was that of a devilish tempter of mankind – of a man who, not content with carrying his crime[s] on his own shoulders, and gaining a livelihood by them, wandered through society to corrupt its honesty and pollute everything that came within his accursed touch.[60]

Ballantine portrayed Agar as a man without a conscience: 'It was nothing to such a man as he that an innocent man should be consigned to a dreadful prison – that would not give him the least pain.'[61]

Fearing, like many others, that Agar had done a deal for his release, Ballantine warned the authorities not to release him in return for the evidence he had given:

No more terrible scourge could be let loose upon society than would flow from the liberation of such a miscreant. At the commission of what baseness would he be likely to hesitate if he thought he might thereby shorten the term of his own incarceration? To secure mercy for himself he would not shrink from destroying the happiness, the reputation, or the liberty of the innocent.[62]

Ballantine also dismissed the notion, proposed by the prosecution and by Agar himself, that Agar had agreed to give evidence out of his sincere concern for the welfare of Fanny:

> The disclosures of Agar had been ascribed to the fact that his compassionate love for that sweet and sentimental young lady, the mother of his child, had been keenly wounded through the unkind treatment she had experienced from Pierce; but when the matter came to be sifted it turned out that [he] had deserted the woman to whom he was so tenderly attached, and had taken up with another, with whom he lived for some time before being taken into custody.[63]

Ballantine went along with Giffard's assertion about Agar's testimony, namely that he was making his story fit his lies: '... [He] fabricated a story based upon certain facts entirely independent of this case, which he easily picked up through his knowledge of Burgess, Tester, and the other officers of the company, and upon these immaterial facts he ... fixed as a means of confirming the accusation against Tester which he had ingeniously engrafted upon them.'[64]

For example, Ballantine explained, Agar had found out that Tester travelled up to Reigate with a black bag 'somewhere about the time' of the commission of the robbery and he then made up 'the untruth that that bag had been taken up by Tester for the express purpose of bringing up the bars of gold'.[65] 'And how was it possible,' Ballantine asked, 'for the prisoner to contradict that statement?'[66] But, he urged the jury to consider:

... if such had been the contents of the black bag ... would [he] have been so foolhardy as to go out of his way to attract observation ... instead of going quietly at once to his own residence and hiding the stolen property? ... he actually went up to the booking-clerk, voluntarily engaged in conversation with him, forced upon his attention the fact that he had been to Reigate and back since office hours, put down the black bag with the bar of gold (as we said) in it, and went away for nearly 10 minutes, leaving the bag behind him until he returned to take his place in the train. No criminal, unless he were positively insane and determined not to escape detection, could have acted in this manner, as Tester was represented to have done.[67]

On the suggestion that Agar and Tester had been seen together frequently and even spotted enjoying tea and wine, Ballantine said that this might be true, but Tester did not know the character of the person with whom he was interacting at that time. According to Ballantine these meetings were merely attempts on Agar's behalf to ingratiate himself with the innocent Tester in order to either corrupt him or, if that proved impossible, to gain information from him. Ballantine declared that Agar used his knowledge of Tester's responsible position in the South Eastern Railway Company to make up the story about him smuggling the key to the safes out of the office for copying. In reality, Ballantine argued, this was an exaggeration of his client's degree of access to the keys: 'It was stated that the keys were sent by Mr Chubb to Mr Brown, the superintendent; and it was reasonable to suppose that the latter gentleman locked them up safely in his own drawer. If he had not done so he would no doubt have been called as a witness to prove the fact.'[68]

As for the accusation that Tester had altered the guard's duty roster in order to ensure that Burgess was working on the mail train when the next valuable transportation of gold was being made, this change could have been carried out quite normally in the course of his work. Agar, Ballantine argued, could have found out that Tester had made a change to the roster that, quite co-incidentally, kept Burgess working on that train for an extra month, and then simply used this information as another way to implicate Tester in the robbery. After all, Ballantine asserted, if the rota was changed, 'the blame for it rested with the superior officer who witnessed ... [Tester] making the alteration....'[69]

Ballantine then turned his attention to the accusations surrounding the division of the spoils from the robbery. According to the evidence presented, he said, 'Tester accepted some Spanish bonds from Agar as his share in the fruits of the crime'. But, Ballantine asked, 'Was it to be believed that Tester would have run the risk of robbing his employers for the sake of two or three Spanish bonds – worth something, perhaps, today, and nothing at all tomorrow...?'[70] The truth of the matter, according to Ballantine, was that Agar had somehow found out that Tester had bought some Spanish bonds, 'and then he tried to make it be believed that Tester got them from him'.[71] This was in order to make it fit in with the rest of his false 'confirmatory evidence'. The story about the six £100 notes was also 'evidently trumped up' to implicate Tester. Ballantine asked why thieves would ever 'change gold, so easily convertible and so difficult to be traced, into banknotes, which afforded so many facilities for detection?'[72] Anyway, he assured the court, 'The notes were never in Tester's hand at all; nor did he write his name upon them. His name had been forged....'[73] After all, he asked them to remember: 'Agar had been a forger all his life – his plots had had their ramifications in America as well as in Europe, and they had extended over more than 20 years, during which period he had contrived almost miraculously to escape detection.'[74]

Throughout his address to the jury, Ballantine portrayed Tester as an innocent man whom Agar was trying to implicate in a crime for his own evil purposes. He 'appealed to the jury not to allow a man who had hitherto borne a high and unimpeachable character to be the victim of the foul machinations of one who sought his ruin'.[75] In the end, everything would depend on whether the jury accepted this portrayal of his client.

CHAPTER 23

No Common Thief

It was three o'clock on the final day of the trial when the judge, Mr Baron Martin, began his summing-up. He began, in deference to his earlier judgement, by making it clear to the members of the jury that Pierce could only be judged on the count of simple larceny. But, he reminded them, this was not the case with Burgess and Tester, as they 'were both servants of the company, and were placed in situations of trust'.[1] Once again he reiterated what had been said by counsel concerning the necessity of disregarding 'all the remarks ... made by the press in reference to this trial'.[2] He stressed to the jury that this was a significant and important case: it was, he said, '... one of the greatest public importance'.[3] In reminding the jury that the case dealt with matters of fidelity and honesty on the part of employees of big companies, he seemed to reveal his own belief in the guilt of Tester and Burgess:

It is one of a class which has unfortunately become very numerous of late, and for which I think the legislature ought speedily to make some special provision, where the great joint-stock companies which have come into existence in such numbers within the last quarter of a century have been plundered by their confidential servants. It seems as though the feeling of attachment and fidelity which ought to exist between clerk and employer is wholly wanted in the case of these companies, and they appear to be regarded as a public spoil.[4]

He then came to the problem of Agar's suitability and reliability as a witness. He accepted that Agar was a professional
thief. But then, he told the court, Burgess and Tester were aware
of that. His comments seemed to raise Agar to the level of master
criminal: 'He was no common thief, however. Before he engaged
in this transaction he was in the possession of £3,000*l* stock,
besides Spanish bonds to the extent of £700*l*....'[5] After all, he
said, the prisoners had only used him in the commission of this
crime because of his impressive skills as a thief: '... he appears to
have been applied to on account of his great professional skill to
undertake this business, just as one would apply to a great physi-
cian or a great lawyer, or any man of great professional
reputation for assistance in his particular walk.'[6]

No matter what sneaking regard the judge seemed to harbour
for Agar's skills, he did agree with earlier comments made
stating that corroboration with Agar's evidence was necessary in
order for it to be accepted. But then he told them:

> If you are convinced from the evidence of other witnesses that
> the story which Agar has told is a true story, if you are of the
> opinion that there are circumstances connected with it which
> must have happened, and which he cannot have invented, and
> that the minute details which he has narrated have been
> corroborated by independent witnesses with whom he can have
> had no communication, and over whom he can have had no
> control, then it is undoubtedly your duty to find the prisoners
> guilty; but, if you have any doubt upon these points, then you
> must acquit them.[7]

He did not personally believe that Agar could have had control
over, or communication with, any of the witnesses, apart from
Fanny Kay: 'Agar was arrested on the 15th August, 1855 ... and
from that time he has had no possible opportunity of making up
a concerted story with anyone, nor indeed is there any one of the
witnesses, except Fanny Kay, who would be likely to enter into
communication with him on the subject.'[8]

Mr Baron Martin also dealt with Agar's motivation for giving evidence, on which he was perfectly clear: 'He is actuated by a violent feeling of animosity against the prisoner Pierce for the breach of trust which he committed in appropriating to himself the £3000 intended for the support of Fanny Kay and the child.'[9] But the judge seemed to want it both ways when he then told the jury that the fact that he had implicated Burgess and Tester, against whom he had 'no feeling of animosity', only made Agar's accusations against them even more credible: '... consider how far he would be likely, if his story were a false one, to inculpate two persons who do not appear to have given him any cause of offence.'[10] While he accepted that neither Pierce nor Tester would have any charge to answer were it not for Agar's testimony, this was not so for Burgess:

> ... there would be evidence to go to the jury even if Agar had not been examined. If you are of the opinion that the robbery took place between London and Folkestone – of which I think the evidence leaves very little doubt – then comes the question how could it have been committed without Burgess's knowledge, seeing that his station was in the compartment in which the gold was carried.[11]

Mr Baron Martin then went through the evidence in detail and looked at it in particular from the viewpoint of the corroboration of Agar's evidence by the other witnesses. He said that Agar's account of the visits to Folkestone with Pierce were backed up by the evidence of Hooker, Hazel, Sharman, Chapman and Ledger: 'Chapman's evidence in particular as to the receipt of the parcel of gold by Agar at Folkestone, and his pretended inability to write a receipt, because of his wounded finger, agreed in every particular with Agar's statement.'[12] Mr Chubb's evidence, he said, confirmed what Agar had said about being told by Tester that one of the keys to the safes had been lost: 'Mr Chubb ... produced the correspondence relating to this transaction, which was in Tester's handwriting, showing that

Tester was acquainted with this circumstance, which it was not likely would have been generally known among the company's servants.'[13] It was also Tester, he said, who arranged that Burgess was 'guard to the mail train so much longer than his regular term of duty (during which time Agar was going up and down the line fitting the key to the safe)....' According to Jones and Russell and, indeed, Agar: 'Tester travelled on the line from Red-hill to London that night, and ... had a little black bag with him.'[14] Continued the judge: 'The waiter at Dover and the porters at the Dover and London stations' corroborated Agar's story about travelling on the 2 a.m. train from Dover to London that night in the company of Pierce. Similarly, Agar's version of melting the gold 'was confirmed ... by Mr Rees, who found the firebricks behind the grate, the burnt flooring at Agar's old residence, and the box of tools at Pierce's'.[15] He was also happy about the corroboration of Agar's evidence concerning the proceeds of the robbery: 'The evidence of the Bank clerks respecting the six £100 notes, and of the stockbrokers, of Lee, the stockjobber, and of Stearn, the publican, were all confirmatory of Agar's evidence as to the division of the plunder.'[16]

Mr Baron Martin's comments had not been at all helpful to the prisoners' cause. How influential his comments would be, no one could tell. Once he had concluded his statement, just before five o'clock, the jury retired to consider its verdict. It depended now on the degree to which the jury had found Agar to be a credible witness, and whether the defence had managed to discredit him sufficiently. Also, was the corroboration of his evidence by the other witnesses strong enough to convict? As it happened, the answer was not long in coming.

CHAPTER 24

As Bad Can Be

———•———

The jury found it necessary to deliberate on the facts of the case for only ten minutes before it returned with a verdict. There was silence in the Old Bailey courtroom as the foreman was called on to announce the decision. He declared that all three defendants had been found guilty; Pierce on the count of simple larceny, and Burgess and Tester on the count of larceny as servants.

Mr Baron Martin addressed the prisoners directly, telling them that they had '... all been convicted, upon pretty nearly the most conclusive evidence which it was possible to lay before a jury....' Once again there seemed to be present in his comments a note of admiration, if not for Edward Agar's character, then at least for his talents:

> The man Agar is a man who is bad, I dare say, as bad can be, but that he is a man of most extraordinary ability no person who heard him examined can for a moment deny. I do not entertain a doubt that it was because he was an old, experienced thief, noted for his extraordinary skill, that he was applied to by you for the purpose of getting this robbery effected ... he is a man of extraordinary talent ... he gave to this and, perhaps, to many other robberies, an amount of care and perseverance, one-tenth of which devoted to honest pursuits must have raised him to a respectable station in life, and ... would probably have enabled him to realize a large fortune.[1]

Nevertheless, said the judge, a life of crime had not served Agar's talents well, and his incarceration and imminent transportation for forgery cut him off from wealth, respect and even sexual gratification: '... instead of being a respected wealthy man, as he might have been, he is a slave for life – separate for ever from all he holds most dear. It is perfectly clear that he was fond of associating with persons of the other sex, but he is entirely cut off from all such associations.'[2] He turned to the suggestion mentioned earlier in the trial that Agar might be granted a pardon in return for giving evidence. He made it clear that that was 'entirely in the breast of the Crown' and that he had 'nothing to do with it'. What is more, in his view, he said, 'it does not follow as a matter of course, that a man of his character will be released from prison because he has given evidence which has had the effect of bringing you to justice'.[3] He said that he had been totally convinced by Agar's testimony:

> He has related to us the various circumstances of this robbery, and has narrated minute details which have been confirmed by upwards of 30 witnesses with whom it was perfectly impossible that he could have had any communication. He could not have told us those details except his story had been a true one; and, for my own part, I believe every word of his evidence from beginning to end.[4]

Mr Baron Martin may have harboured a sneaking regard for Agar, but he was not impressed at all by the character or talents of Pierce. He went on, rather bizarrely, to criticize Pierce for what he had done to Agar and Fanny:

> You had been long connected with this man Agar; he trusted you, and he gave you £3,000 stock to be invested for the benefit of his child and its mother, together with £600, his share of the produce of this robbery, and the rest of the gold which had not been sold. In all you must have got out of him about £15,000. This you stole and appropriated to your own

use. It is a worse offence, I declare, than the act of which you have just been found guilty. I would rather have been concerned in stealing the gold than in the robbery of that wretched woman, - call her harlot, if you will, - and her child. A greater villain than you are, I believe does not exist.[5]

The crowd assembled in court obviously agreed with these sentiments as they broke out in spontaneous applause.

The judge regretted, he continued, not being able to impose a heavier sentence on Pierce: 'I am unfortunately compelled to inflict a punishment less severe than upon the other prisoners. They were servants of the company, and you were not.' He admitted that he had even been tempted to interpret the law in a rather unconventional way in order to subject Pierce to a more appropriate penalty, but in the end had decided against it: 'By a strained construction of the law you might, perhaps, have been got into the same category with the other two; but I am unwilling, and my brother Willes agrees with me, to strain the law against you.'

So it was that Pierce, the instigator of the whole plan, the man who had first come up with the idea of robbing the train in transit, and the corrupter of both Burgess and Tester, received the lightest sentence: he was to be imprisoned for a period of two years with hard labour, three months of which – the first, the twelfth and the twenty-fourth – were to be served in solitary confinement. Samuel Smiles of the South Eastern Railway, like a great many other people, thought that this sentence was too light.[6] A similar view was expressed in an article published in *The Times*, where this notion of Pierce as the principal villain was evident along with some admiration for Agar:

Agar ... had invested the proceeds of his many crimes for the benefit of a woman whom he seems to have loved with all the fondness of which such a man was capable. Pierce was his trustee, and Pierce, like a true thief, betrayed his trust. The woman was left destitute, and her paramour, the hardened felon whom no scruples of conscience would have moved, denounced the half-forgotten robbery from his cell at Portland. None of our readers will fail to sympathise with the manly indignation with which Baron Martin denounced the villainy of Pierce, or to share his regret that the sentence of the law falls lightest on the basest of the villains....'[7]

Such articles reflected an image of Agar as the romantic villain with a kind heart, but tended to minimize his long history of serious crime, his pivotal role in the train robbery itself and his many infidelities towards Fanny.

If Pierce had got off lightly, however, the same was not true of Burgess and Tester. They sat 'without out any change of demeanour' as the time arrived for the judge to address them:

> ... Burgess and Tester, there is no manner of doubt that your case is that – not infrequent of late – of men who, having good characters and being placed by your employers in situations of trust, were unable to resist the temptation of getting possession of a large sum of money all at once. Whether Agar tempted you or whether you were tempted by Pierce, as is most likely, and that then Agar was applied to as a man noted for his skill and ability in such matters, it is impossible for us to know now. That you Burgess, a man who had been 15 years in the service of the company, and were receiving good wages, and that you Tester, the son of a most respectable man, should have yielded to this temptation, is greatly to be deplored; but we should be departing from our duty to the public ... if we did not visit you with the severest punishment. You were willing to play the game, and you must pay the forfeit.[8]

Once again the judge's comments regarding Agar were relatively favourable:

> The learned counsel who have addressed the jury on your behalf have spoken in the strongest terms of Agar's character.

No doubt he deserves all they have said, but let it be said in his favour that he remained true to you, that he said not a word about this robbery until he heard of Pierce's base conduct. As he gave his evidence he did not appear to feel towards you that bitter animosity which was so clearly manifested in him, and, I must say, not unnaturally, under the circumstances, towards Pierce. He had no motive to accuse you falsely, and this to my mind is an additional proof of the truth of his story.

Finally, he came specifically to the sentence to be visited on them: 'The sentence of this court upon you, Burgess and Tester, is that you be severally transported beyond the seas for the term of 14 years.'

Tester's friends, who had advised him to return to England and hand himself over to the law, were particularly shocked by the severity of the sentence handed down.[9] Tester himself was visibly shaken: '… he appeared completely overpowered, and it was with difficulty that he seemed to recover himself sufficiently to walk away from the bar without assistance.'[10]

The convicted prisoners were taken down but, before proceedings came to an end, Bodkin entered a petition asking that the Turkish bonds that had been bought by Pierce using Agar's money should now be awarded to the South Eastern Railway Company. The judge said that he could not rule then and there on the matter, but his own preference was that these bonds, 'which had been clearly purchased with the money entrusted to the prisoner by Agar', should be given to Fanny Kay and the child.[11] Bodkin assured him that 'the company had no desire to take possession of any property which was not the produce of the robbery'.[12] The judge, therefore, asked that the company 'specify on affidavit what property they thought themselves entitled to' and said that 'he and Mr Justice Willes would then make whatever order seemed right to them under the circumstances'.[13]

In the weeks that followed a number of interested parties began to battle over these Turkish bonds. Some argued that

Agar's claim that he had arranged for his assets to be used to support Fanny and the child was just another clever scam of his. It was intended, the argument went, to ensure that Fanny would get possession of the money from the robbery. If he could get a pardon in return for giving evidence, then they could both go off and enjoy the money together. *The Times* of 17 January 1857 printed a report stating that the court had denied the claim from the railway company for Agar's Turkish bonds and that they had already been granted to Fanny Kay.[14] This award to the value of £2,500 would, according to the correspondent, 'enable her to lead an easy and, if so inclined, reputable life'.[15] However, this inaccurate report was quickly rebutted by a letter, published in the newspaper on 20 January, from Alexander Crosley, the under-sheriff of London and Middlesex and one of the claimants to the assets. The under-sheriff made readers aware that no decision had yet been made regarding Agar's wealth.

Several affidavits were laid before the judges, and a number of hearings on the matter were held in January 1857, again under the adjudication of Mr Baron Martin. On 27 January, all the interested parties appeared before Mr Baron Martin and Mr Justice Willes at the Exchequer Chamber in Westminster.[16] Mr Sleigh, counsel for the sheriffs of London and Middlesex, claimed that according to legal precedent the money should be awarded to the city: '... from time immemorial the property of the prisoners convicted at the Old Bailey had been given up to the sheriffs ... and this was the first time that their rights in this respect had ever been contested ... the court had no power under such circumstances to order the property to be given to Fanny Kay.'[17] In an incredible act of audacity, a claim was also submitted on behalf of the recently arrested barrister, Saward, for £260, which he said he was owed 'for costs that had been incurred ... in conducting some legal proceedings for ... Pierce'.[18] Tester's wife, through her legal representative, also claimed some of her husband's Spanish bonds. Both claims were rejected out of hand.[19] Bodkin, for the South Eastern Railway Company, argued that the company had the right to have repaid to it 'that which was clearly ... the produce of the stolen property'. He said that, so far, the company had paid out £10,000 in compensation for the stolen gold, and that since these funds were obviously a produce of the crime the company was 'clearly entitled to this money'. Sleigh, on behalf of the sheriffs, said that they would have no objection to the railway company receiving a fair amount, as long as they were rewarded the remainder.

Mr Reynolds, the solicitor for the Treasury, contradicted this automatic right to the property of prisoners that was being claimed by the sheriffs on behalf of the city: '... under ordinary circumstances the property of a felon was taken possession of by the Crown, but it was never retained when any persons made out a good case for its restoration. In some instances it had been restored to the felon himself for good conduct, and also to his wife....'[20] The Treasury, said Reynolds, '... always endeavoured to act according to the equity of each case'.[21]

Notwithstanding all these conflicting claims, it was evident that Baron Martin was still inclined to award the assets to Fanny Kay. She had, he said, 'an equitable right to the property, according to the request of Agar'.[22]

In the end, after much discussion, it was determined by the court that the South Eastern Railway Company should be granted that portion of Agar's wealth determined to be the proceeds of the train robbery and that the rest be granted, for the time being, into the safe keeping of the Commissioner of the Metropolitan Police, Sir Richard Mayne, until further orders could be made regarding it. The railway company were to receive five-sixths of it.[23] Then, some weeks later, Mr Baron Martin made out an order granting the remaining money to Fanny:

Late on Monday evening Mr Clark, the clerk of the Central Criminal Court, received a communication from Mr Baron Martin directing him to make out an order upon Sir Richard Mayne for the Turkish bonds that were found in the possession of Pearce [sic], one of the bullion robbers, to be delivered up to

Mr Rees, the solicitor to the South Eastern Railway, in trust for the benefit of Fanny Kay and her child.[24]

Sadly for Fanny, this was not the end of the matter. Other court battles followed until, finally, Mr Baron Martin's decision to make that award to Fanny was overturned on the grounds that he had no legal power to make it: '... a rule had been granted to quash an order made by the judges at the Central Criminal Court, whereby certain Turkish bonds in the possession of the police were ordered to be delivered up, and a portion of them ... to be settled in trust for one Fanny Kay and her infant child.'[25] The order regarding Fanny's share of the money had been duly quashed and she was now excluded. The matter was referred, however, to the Law and Parliamentary Committee for final adjudication.

In the direct aftermath of the trial, other legal battles ensued. Despite the claim made by the South Eastern Railway Company that they had paid out £10,000 in compensation for the gold that had been stolen, Henry Abel was still not happy with the way in which he had been treated. On 20 March 1857, he wrote to the secretary of the South Eastern Railway, Samuel Smiles, asking that they settle a claim arising from the non delivery of the contents of his package marked 'P.D. 184': '... my correspondents in Paris inform me that they have had a claim made upon them by Messrs. Caillard and Co., for the carriage of P.D. 184, dispatched by me on the 15th May, 1855, to Paris *via* South Eastern Railway.'[26] Messrs Caillard & Co. were demanding 141 francs, or £5 12s 10d, from Abel. Abel was quite direct on the matter and alluded to the involvement of the South Eastern Railway's own employees in the robbery. He said that he was not prepared to pay for the transportation of lead shot: 'This is the box from which your servants abstracted my gold, substituting lead ... I presume your directors will hardly deem it fair that I should pay carriage upon your lead, and not upon my own gold.'[27] He asked that the South Eastern Railway cover the charge. The South Eastern Railway, however, repre-

sented by Mr W. Eborall, manager, were far from helpful: '...
the request you make for this company to pay such claim,' the
manager wrote, 'I beg leave to inform you we cannot in any way
interfere in the matter.'[28] Abel was so outraged by this response
that he sent the correspondence to the press for publication.

As for the perpetrators of the crime, their fate had been
decided. Pierce was taken away to serve his two years of hard
labour in England. Burgess and Tester had allowed themselves,
primarily through greed, to be lured into committing a serious
crime, and they now faced a serious penalty. They were exiled
from England on 26 August 1858, sailing from Plymouth
Harbour on board the *Edwin Fox* bound for the Swan River
Colony in Western Australia. Eighty-six days later their ship
docked in Fremantle and they had both managed to survive the
gruelling trip.

In the end neither Burgess nor Tester served as long as their
sentences had suggested they would. Burgess, convict number
5203, served his sentence in confinement until, on 21 December
1859, he received his ticket of leave. Under the ticket of leave
system a prisoner, on the grounds of good behaviour, would be
released from captivity early, as long as he agreed to remain
within a specified geographical area. He would be permitted to
work, purchase property and even marry. On 21 March 1862,
Burgess was granted a conditional pardon under which he
regained his freedom but was not yet permitted to return to
England.[29] Meanwhile Tester, convict number 5204, got his
ticket of leave on 14 July 1859. On 17 October 1861, he was
granted a conditional pardon. According to the prison records
he sailed on the *York* in 1863, presumably back to England, and
into historical obscurity.[30]

For a time, rumours abounded that Agar would receive a
pardon from his sentence for forgery in return for his part in
bringing the other three perpetrators of the Great Train Robbery
to justice. At the end of the trial at the Old Bailey, Bodkin intimated to Mr Baron Martin that he wished to say something
regarding this question of Agar's release from his current

sentence. He felt it was only fair to Mr Rees, he said, 'to mention that, when he [Rees] saw Agar at Portland, he had distinctly stated to him that he was not to expect any remission of his sentence in return for the evidence which he had consented to give'.[31] However, many people did not believe this, and reports in the newspapers claimed, 'on good authority', that Agar was about to receive a pardon on condition that he left the country and did not return:

'It appears to be probable that the Government will grant a pardon to Edward Agar, the approver in the case of Pierce, Burgess, and Tester for the bullion robbery upon the South Eastern Railway. The pardon, however, will only be a conditional one, and the condition will be, that the convict shall leave this country, and care will be taken to enforce this condition.'[32]

He was to get this concession, the reports claimed, not because of the evidence he had given against his colleagues, but because 'he really was not guilty of the forgery for which he was convicted ... and that the transaction was a "plant" upon him, for the purpose of getting him out of the way'.[33] The newspapers had grave doubts about this claim of innocence, as it had all the appearances of a convenient excuse for his release. With all these rumours of an imminent pardon for Agar, many were still far from happy with a situation in which Fanny could yet be granted a substantial portion of the money that had come from criminal activity and Agar could be granted his freedom:

... the effect would be that Agar and his mistress would obtain possession of the whole of the produce of a long career of plunder, and the former would have the full enjoyment of his ill-gotten gains.[34]

It was evident that the supposed wish expressed by Agar, that the money should be used for the benefit of Fanny Kay and her child, was merely suggested for the purpose of enabling him to regain possession of his ill-gotten plunder, the result of a life of the most extraordinary iniquity, in the event of his being acquitted when he was tried for forgery, and should he now obtain a conditional pardon, which it is considered very probable may be granted to him, the result would be that he and Fanny Kay would walk off with nearly £3,000 in money, the whole being, as before stated, the produce of crime.[35]

It was reported in February, 1857, however, that Agar was still in custody:

The convict Edward Agar, who gave evidence against his accomplices in this extraordinary robbery, has been sent back to his old quarters at Portland Prison, and no intimation has as yet been given on the part of the government of any intention to commute his original sentence of transportation for life, and he has to perform the same labour as the other convicts who are under a similar sentence.

In the end, all this talk of a pardon came to nothing, and on 23 September 1857 Agar, like his accomplices Burgess and Tester, was transported to Australia on board the 763-ton ship the *Nile*. He was assigned the convict number 4580. The records show that on 17 September 1860 he was granted a ticket of leave, and on 13 September 1867 a conditional pardon. In 1869 Edward Agar sailed for Colombo in Ceylon and no more was heard of him.

Meanwhile the criminal empire of Agar's old accomplice, Saward, had fallen apart. His two 'employees', Hardwicke and Attwell, were tried at the Old Bailey on 27 October 1856. The evidence was stacking up against them so much during the trial that midway through Hardwicke asked to change his plea from not guilty to guilty. Bodkin, however, on behalf of the prosecution, insisted 'that as the jury were charged, the proper course would be to take a verdict of guilty at the close of the case'.[36] In the end they were both found guilty of forgery and sentenced to transportation for life. A few weeks later they testified in court against their old boss, Saward, and his right-hand man,

Anderson. As a result Saward and Anderson were also convicted and sentenced to transportation for life.

The arrests and conviction of both Saward and Agar were, before long, being seen to have had a positive effect on crime levels in London:

'It is a satisfaction ... to know that, during the last two years, the offence of forgery, upon a great scale, has very much diminished, and this is very materially owing to the conviction of Saward, the barrister – well known in flash circles as 'Jem, the Penman'....[37]

Saward and Agar were complete 'artists' in forgery, and it is calculated that since their conviction the amount lost by the London bankers, by forgery, has diminished to at least the extent of ten thousand a year; so that although the conviction of these two individuals cost a very large sum of money, it was very well expended in getting rid of such dangerous characters. Since they have been disposed of, it appears that no one among the ranks of offenders of this description has been clever enough to supply their place....[38]

Sadly, the conditions of Fanny Kay's life did not improve. In December 1861 the Law and Parliamentary Committee, which had been charged with deciding what to do with Agar's assets, announced that Fanny Kay had died. It became known that Fanny 'had made a will devising her interest to her child'.[39] In deference to the plight of the child, the Committee agreed that '... the corporation should forego its claim to the property, and allow it to be used for the purposes named in the will of the deceased woman Fanny Kay, namely, for the benefit of her child'.[40] Agar's money had finally made its way to his son.

The story of the Great Train Robbery was at an end. Pierce, Agar, Burgess and Tester had the dubious honour of being the pioneers of a new type of crime, but others would follow. Their influence was felt not only in Britain, but around the world, as reports such as the following from France demonstrate: 'Gold Robbery on a French Railway. – ... at the beginning of last week, a parcel of 16,000f, in specie, which was being transported from the office of the Messageries Generales to the railway station, disappeared before arriving at the latter. Three individuals suspected of the theft have been since arrested.'[41]

For its part, the South Eastern Railway Company, like all other railway companies, was forced to review its security procedures. From the time of the Great Train Robbery on, only purpose-built bullion vans, not ordinary guards' vans, were used to transport gold and other valuable cargoes. A fit for purpose strong-house was built at Folkestone for safes to be kept in on arrival.[42] There was no mistaking it, the era of train robbery had begun, and Agar, Pierce, Burgess and Tester were assured their infamous places in history. One writer in 1859 was still marvelling at the audacity of their crime and the fantastic nature of its discovery: 'The acute cunning with which it was planned ... the careful painstaking with which all the preliminaries were carried out – the wonderful skill with which the actual robbery was effected – and the curious way in which it was discovered, these circumstances combined make the gold robbery stand out in bold relief....'[43]

Select Bibliography

Transcripts of all the trials that took place at the Central Criminal Court can be found in *The Proceedings of the Old Bailey*, available on-line at www.oldbaileyonline.org:

Edward Agar, 22 October 1855
William Pierce, James Burgess and William George Tester, 5 January 1857
William Salt Hardwicke and Henry Attwell, 27 October 1856
James Townsend Saward and James Anderson, 2 March 1857
William Nash, 13 June 1853

Newspapers:

The Times
Daily News
Morning Chronicle
Caledonian Mercury
Freeman's Journal and Daily Commercial Advertiser
Glasgow Herald
Hampshire Telegraph and Sussex Chronicle
Jackson's Oxford Journal
Liverpool Mercury
Lloyd's Weekly Newspaper
Birmingham Daily Post
North Wales Chronicle
News of the World
Northern Echo
Reynold's Newspaper
Aberdeen Journal

Belfast Newsletter
Bristol Mercury
Era
Examiner
Hull Packet and East Riding Times
Ipswich Journal
Leeds Mercury
Preston Guardian
Trewman's Exeter Flying Post or Plymouth and Cornish Advertiser

Published Sources:

Cruikshank, P., *A Full Report of the Trial of Pierce, Burgess and Tester for the Great Gold Robbery* (H. Vickers and Read & Co, 1856)

Evans, D.M., *Facts, Failures and Frauds: Revelations, Financial, Mercantile, Criminal* (Groombridge, 1859)

Fido, M. and Skinner, K., *The Official Encyclopaedia of Scotland Yard* (Virgin Publishing, 2000)

Fletcher, J., 'The First Great Train Robbery (*The Journal of the Railway and Canal*, 26; 3; 1980)

Gay, W.O., 'A Brilliant Crime: The Great Train Robbery 1855' (*British Transport Police Journal*)

Mackay, T. (Ed.), *The Autobiography of Samuel Smiles, LL.D.* (E.P. Dutton & Co., New York, 1905)

Maycock, W., Sir, *Celebrated Crimes and Criminals* (The Temple Company, 1890)

Measom, G., *The Official Guide to the South Eastern Railway and its Branches* (W.H. Smith & Son, 1853)

Oates, J., *Great Train Crimes: Murder and Robbery on the Railways* (Wharncliffe Books, 2010)

Robbins, M., 'The Great South-Eastern Bullion Robbery', (*The Railway Magazine*, May 1955, pp.315-317)

Sekon, G.A. (Nokes, G.A.), *The History of the South Eastern Railway* (London, 1895)

'The Great Train Robbery' (*Steam Scene*, Newsletter of the Steam Tram and Railway Preservation (Co-op) Society Ltd, Vol. 4, Issue 6, December. 2007)

Notes

NOTE: Where I have directly quoted from contemporary accounts, in the interest of simplicity and where it does not alter the meaning, I have, on a few occasions, altered the spelling capitalization and punctuation.

Chapter 1: London to Dover

1 Measom, p.vii.
2 Measom, p.vii.
3 Measom, p.vii.
4 Old Bailey Proceedings Online (www.oldbaileyonline.org), January. 1857, trial of Pierce, Burgess and Tester, (t18570105-250) (hereafter referred to as 'Trial of Pierce, Burgess and Tester'), Testimony of Sellins.
5 Trial of Pierce, Burgess and Tester, Testimony of Abel; For the value, *Morning Chronicle*, 9 June 1855, reporting on the hearing into Samuel Seal.
6 Trial of Pierce, Burgess and Tester.
7 He said he thought it was '26, Rue Rivoli', *Morning Chronicle*, 9 June 1855 reporting on the hearing into Samuel Seal.
8 Letter to *Daily News*, 16 January 1857, from Adam Spielman & Co; *Morning Chronicle*, 9 June 1855 reporting on the hearing into Samuel Seal.
9 Trial of Pierce, Burgess and Tester, Testimony of Chaplin.
10 Measom, p.8.
11 Trial of Pierce, Burgess and Tester, Testimony of Chaplin.
12 *The Times*, 14 January 1857.
13 Trial of Pierce, Burgess and Tester, Testimony of Cox.
14 Trial of Pierce, Burgess and Tester.
15 Trial of Pierce, Burgess and Tester, Testimony of Cox.
16 Trial of Pierce, Burgess and Tester, Testimony of Bailey.
17 Trial of Pierce, Burgess and Tester, Testimony of Kennedy.

Chapter 2: The Same as Any Other Night

1 Trial of Pierce, Burgess and Tester, Testimony of Kennedy.
2 Trial of Pierce, Burgess and Tester, Testimony of Golder.
3 *The Times*, 14 January 1857.
4 Trial of Pierce, Burgess and Tester, Testimony of Golder; *The Times*, 14 January 18 January 1857.
5 Trial of Pierce, Burgess and Tester, Testimony of Major.
6 Trial of Pierce, Burgess and Tester, Testimony of Everard.
7 Trial of Pierce, Burgess and Tester, Testimony of Major.
8 Trial of Pierce, Burgess and Tester, Testimony of Major.
9 Trial of Pierce, Burgess and Tester, Testimony of Major.
10 Trial of Pierce, Burgess and Tester, Testimony of Major.
11 Trial of Pierce, Burgess and Tester.

Chapter 3: Feloniously Abstracted

1 *The Autobiography of Samuel Smiles*, p.200.
2 *The Times*, 22 May 1855; *Lloyd's Weekly Newspaper*, 27 May 1855.
3 *The Times*, 21 May 1855.
4 Trial of Pierce, Burgess and Tester, Testimony of Witherden.
5 Trial of Pierce, Burgess and Tester, Testimony of Williams and Witherden.
6 Trial of Pierce, Burgess and Tester, Testimony of Dickenson.
7 *The Times*, 15 December 1856, Testimony of Woodhouse given at the Mansion House.
8 Trial of Pierce, Burgess and Tester, Testimony of Dickenson.
9 Trial of Pierce, Burgess and Tester, Testimony of Dickenson.

Chapter 4: The Investigation

1 *The Autobiography of Samuel Smiles* p.198.
2 *The Times*, 24 March 1849.
3 Trial of Pierce, Burgess and Tester, Testimony of Abel.
4 Laxton, W., *The Civil Engineer and Architect's Journal* (W. Ken & Co, 1866).
5 *Lloyd's Weekly Newspaper*, 27 May 1855.
6 *Lloyd's Weekly Newspaper*, 3 June 1855.
7 *Lloyd's Weekly Newspaper*, 3 June 1855.
8 *Lloyd's Weekly Newspaper*, 3 June 1855.
9 *Lloyd's Weekly Newspaper*, 3 June 1855.
10 *Lloyd's Weekly Newspaper*, 3 June 1855.
11 *Daily News*, 28 May 1855.
12 *Daily News*, 28 May 1855.
13 *Morning Chronicle*, 28 May 1855.

14 *Daily News, 28 May 1855.*
15 *Daily News*, 28 May 1855.
16 *Morning Chronicle*, 28 May 1855.
17 *Lloyd's Weekly Newspaper*, 17 May 1855.
18 *Lloyd's Weekly Newspaper*, 17 May 1855; *Morning Chronicle*, 28 May 1855.
19 *Lloyd's Weekly Newspaper*, 17 May 1855; *Morning Chronicle*, 28 May 1855.
20 *Lloyd's Weekly Newspaper*, 27 May 1855.
21 *Lloyd's Weekly Newspaper*, 27 May 1855.
22 *Daily News*, 28 May 1855.
23 *Morning Chronicle*, 9 June 1855.
24 *Daily News*, 18 June 1855.
25 *The Autobiography of Samuel Smiles*, p.199.
26 *The Autobiography of Samuel Smiles*, p.199.
27 *The Autobiography of Samuel Smiles*, p.201.
28 *The Autobiography of Samuel Smiles*, p.201.
29 *The Times*, 3 December 1856.
30 *The Autobiography of Samuel Smiles*, p.199.
31 *The Autobiography of Samuel Smiles*, p.199.
32 *News of the World*, 30 November 1856.

Chapter Five: Dishonour Among Thieves

 1 Born in 1817 according to Fremantle Prison Records, available at www.fremantleprison.com.au.
 2 *The Autobiography of Samuel Smiles*, p.206.
 3 Fremantle Prison Records show him as 'semi-literate', see www.fremantleprison.com.au.
 4 *The Times*, 27 November 1856; *Daily News*, 26 November 1856.
 5 *Daily News*, 26 November 1856.
 6 *Daily News*, 26 November 1856; Old Bailey Proceedings (www.oldbaileyonline.org), June 1853, trial of Nash (t18530613-723).
 7 Old Bailey Proceedings (www.oldbaileyonline.org), June 1853, trial of Nash, (t18530613-723).
 8 *Daily News*, 26 November 1856.
 9 *Daily News*, 26 November 1856.
10 Fanny's middle name was 'Bolam' according to the record of her son's baptism in July, 1855, Church of England Parish Registers, 1754–1906, even though it was given as 'Bolan' in *The Times*, 18 November 1856, and Trial of Pierce, Burgess and Tester, and as 'Poland' in *The Times*, 15 January 1857.
11 *The Times*, 18 November 1856.
12 According to herself, *The Times*, 18 November 1856.

13   See most of these mentioned in *The Times*, 18 November 1856.

14   Church of England Parish Registers, 1754–1906, Parish of St Giles
     Cripplegate, London, under name of 'Ager'. The child was born on 7
     July, 1854 and baptised on 1 July, 1855.

15   Old Bailey Proceedings (www.oldbaileyonline.org), October 1855, trial
     of Agar, (t18551022-943).

16   Old Bailey Proceedings (www.oldbaileyonline.org), October 1855, trial
     of Agar, (t18551022-943).

17   Old Bailey Proceedings (www.oldbaileyonline.org), October 1855, trial
     of Agar, (t18551022-943).

18   Old Bailey Proceedings (www.oldbaileyonline.org), October 1855, trial
     of Agar, (t18551022-943).

19   Old Bailey Proceedings (www.oldbaileyonline.org), October 1855, trial
     of Agar, (t18551022-943).

20   Old Bailey Proceedings (www.oldbaileyonline.org), October 1855, trial
     of Agar, (t18551022-943).

21   Old Bailey Proceedings (www.oldbaileyonline.org), October 1855, trial
     of Agar, (t18551022-943).

22   Old Bailey Proceedings (www.oldbaileyonline.org), October 1855, trial
     of Agar, (t18551022-943).

23   Old Bailey Proceedings (www.oldbaileyonline.org), October 1855, trial
     of Agar, (t18551022-943).

24   Old Bailey Proceedings (www.oldbaileyonline.org), October 1855, trial
     of Agar, (t18551022-943).

25   Old Bailey Proceedings (www.oldbaileyonline.org), October 1855, trial
     of Agar, (t18551022-943).

26   Old Bailey Proceedings (www.oldbaileyonline.org), October 1855, trial
     of Agar, (t18551022-943).

27   Old Bailey Proceedings (www.oldbaileyonline.org), October 1855, trial
     of Agar, (t18551022-943).

28   Old Bailey Proceedings (www.oldbaileyonline.org), October 1855, trial
     of Agar, (t18551022-943).

29   Old Bailey Proceedings (www.oldbaileyonline.org), October 1855, trial
     of Agar, (t18551022-943).

30   Old Bailey Proceedings (www.oldbaileyonline.org), October 1855, trial
     of Agar, (t18551022-943).

31   Old Bailey Proceedings (www.oldbaileyonline.org), October 1855, trial
     of Agar, (t18551022-943).

32   Old Bailey Proceedings (www.oldbaileyonline.org), October 1855, trial
     of Agar, (t18551022-943).

33   Old Bailey Proceedings (www.oldbaileyonline.org), October 1855, trial
     of Agar, (t18551022-943).

34   Old Bailey Proceedings (www.oldbaileyonline.org), October 1855, trial
     of Agar, (t18551022-943).

35 Old Bailey Proceedings (www.oldbaileyonline.org), October 1855, trial of Agar, (t18551022-943).
36 Old Bailey Proceedings (www.oldbaileyonline.org), October 1855, trial of Agar, (t18551022-943).
37 Old Bailey Proceedings (www.oldbaileyonline.org), October 1855, trial of Agar, (t18551022-943).
38 Old Bailey Proceedings (www.oldbaileyonline.org), October 1855, trial of Agar, (t18551022-943).
39 Old Bailey Proceedings (www.oldbaileyonline.org), October 1855, trial of Agar, (t18551022-943).
40 Old Bailey Proceedings (www.oldbaileyonline.org), October 1855, trial of Agar, (t18551022-943).
41 Old Bailey Proceedings (www.oldbaileyonline.org), October 1855, trial of Agar, (t18551022-943).
42 Old Bailey Proceedings (www.oldbaileyonline.org), October 1855, trial of Agar, (t18551022-943).
43 Old Bailey, 22 October 1855.
44 Old Bailey Proceedings (www.oldbaileyonline.org), October 1855, trial of Agar, (t18551022-943), Testimony of Forrester.
45 Trial of Pierce, Burgess and Tester, Testimony of Agar.
46 *Daily News*, 14 January 1857.
47 Trial of Pierce, Burgess and Tester, Testimony of Agar.
48 *Daily News*, 14 January 1857.
49 Old Bailey Proceedings (www.oldbaileyonline.org), October 1855, trial of Agar, (t18551022-943) Testimony of Smith and Forrester.
50 Old Bailey Proceedings (www.oldbaileyonline.org), October 1855, trial of Agar, (t18551022-943) Testimony of Forrester.

Chapter 6: A Fearful Representation

1 Old Bailey Proceedings (www.oldbaileyonline.org), October 1855, trial of Agar, (t18551022-943).
2 Old Bailey Proceedings (www.oldbaileyonline.org), October 1855, trial of Agar, (t18551022-943).
3 Old Bailey Proceedings (www.oldbaileyonline.org), October 1855, trial of Agar, (t18551022-943).
4 Old Bailey Proceedings (www.oldbaileyonline.org), October 1855, trial of Agar, (t18551022-943).
5 Old Bailey Proceedings (www.oldbaileyonline.org), October 1855, trial of Agar, (t18551022-943).
6 Old Bailey Proceedings (www.oldbaileyonline.org), October 1855, trial of Agar, (t18551022-943).
7 Old Bailey Proceedings (www.oldbaileyonline.org), October 1855, trial of Agar, (t18551022-943).

8 Old Bailey Proceedings (www.oldbaileyonline.org), October 1855, trial of Agar, (t18551022-943).
9 Old Bailey Proceedings (www.oldbaileyonline.org), October 1855, trial of Agar, (t18551022-943).
10 Old Bailey Proceedings (www.oldbaileyonline.org), October 1855, trial of Agar, (t18551022-943).
11 *Daily News*, 26 November 1856.
12 *Daily News*, 26 November 1856.
13 Old Bailey Proceedings (www.oldbaileyonline.org), October 1855, trial of Agar, (t18551022-943).
14 *The Autobiography of Samuel Smiles*, p.201
15 *The Autobiography of Samuel Smiles*, p.201.

Chapter 7: An Original but Criminal Idea

1 He suffered with lumbago, according to Fanny's testimony given at the trial of Pierce, Burgess and Tester, and had a 'broad Lancashire dialect'
2 *Glasgow Herald*, 28 November 1856.
3 *Daily News*, 10 January 1857.
4 Trial of Pierce, Burgess and Tester, Testimony of Agar.
5 Trial of Pierce, Burgess and Tester, Testimony of Agar.
6 Trial of Pierce, Burgess and Tester, Testimony of Agar.
7 *The Times*, 12 January 1857.
8 Agar's testimony at the Mansion House, *Daily News*, 14 November 1856.
9 Eight and a half years, according to a letter written by Samuel Smiles, quoted in *The Times*, 9 December 1856.
10 *Daily News*, 11 December 1856; *Morning Chronicle*, 11 December 1856.
11 *Daily News*, 11 December 1856.
12 Trial of Pierce, Burgess and Tester, Testimony of Agar.
13 Trial of Pierce, Burgess and Tester, Testimony of Agar, *The Times*, 11 December 1856, Mansion House.
14 *The Times* 14 January 1857.
15 Trial of Pierce, Burgess and Tester, Testimony of Hooker.
16 Trial of Pierce, Burgess and Tester, Testimony of Hazel; *Daily News*, 15 December 1856, Mansion House.
17 Trial of Pierce, Burgess and Tester, Testimony of Hooker; *Daily News*, 11 December 1856, Mansion House.
18 *Daily News*, 11 December 1856, Mansion House.
19 *The Times*, 14 January 1857.
20 Trial of Pierce, Burgess and Tester, Testimony of Agar, it was near St Mary's Church in Dover, according to Trial of Pierce, Burgess and Tester, Testimony of Werter Clark.

21 Trial of Pierce, Burgess and Tester, Testimony of Agar.
22 Trial of Pierce, Burgess and Tester, Testimony of Agar.
23 Trial of Pierce, Burgess and Tester, Testimony of Agar.
24 Trial of Pierce, Burgess and Tester, Testimony of Agar.

Chapter 8: The Intervention of Luck

1 Trial of Pierce, Burgess and Tester, Testimony of Chubb.
2 Trial of Pierce, Burgess and Tester, Testimony of Chubb.
3 Trial of Pierce, Burgess and Tester, Testimony of Chubb.
4 *Daily News*, 14 November 1856.
5 Trial of Pierce, Burgess and Tester, Testimony of Agar.
6 Value from Specie and Finance Way Bill.
7 *The Times*, 11 December 1856; Evans p.488.
8 Trial of Pierce, Burgess and Tester, Testimony of Agar, date from Specie and Finance Way Bill.
9 *Morning Chronicle*, 11 December 1856, Testimony of Chapman at the Mansion House.
10 Trial of Pierce, Burgess and Tester, Testimony of Hazel.
11 Trial of Pierce, Burgess and Tester, Testimony of Sharman.
12 *The Times*, 14 January 1857.
13 Trial of Pierce, Burgess and Tester, Testimony of Hazel.
14 Trial of Pierce, Burgess and Tester, Testimony of Agar.
15 According to the Testimony of Agar at the Mansion House, *Daily News*, 14 November 1856.
16 Trial of Pierce, Burgess and Tester, Testimony of Agar.
17 *The Times*, 14 January 1857.
18 Trial of Pierce, Burgess and Tester, Testimony of Porter.
19 Trial of Pierce, Burgess and Tester, Testimony of Agar.
20 Trial of Pierce, Burgess and Tester, Testimony of Agar.
21 Trial of Pierce, Burgess and Tester, Testimony of Agar.
22 Trial of Pierce, Burgess and Tester, Testimony of Agar.
23 Agar, testimony given at the Mansion House, *Daily News*, 14 November 1856.
24 Trial of Pierce, Burgess and Tester, Testimony of Agar.
25 'Or something to that effect,' according to Trial of Pierce, Burgess and Tester, Testimony of Knight.
26 Trial of Pierce, Burgess and Tester, Testimony of Agar; *The Times*, 17 January 1857.
27 Trial of Pierce, Burgess and Tester, Testimony of Agar.
28 *The Times*, 14 November 1856; *The Times*, 14 January 1857; Trial of Pierce, Burgess and Tester, Testimony of Agar; *Glasgow Herald*, 17 November 1856.
29 Trial of Pierce, Burgess and Tester, Testimony of Agar.

30 Trial of Pierce, Burgess and Tester, Testimony of Agar.
31 *The Times*, 14 January 1857; *Daily News*, 14 November 1856.
32 *Daily News*, 14 November 1856.
33 Trial of Pierce, Burgess and Tester, Testimony of Agar.

Chapter 9: The First Train Robbery in History

1 *The Times*, 14 November 1856, the Mansion House; *Daily News*, 14 November, 1856.
2 *Daily News*, 14 November 1856.
3 Trial of Pierce, Burgess and Tester, Testimony of Honnor.
4 Trial of Pierce, Burgess and Tester, Testimony of Agar.
5 *Daily News*, 14 November 1856; Trial of Pierce, Burgess and Tester, Testimony of Agar.
6 Trial of Pierce, Burgess and Tester, Testimony of Agar.
7 Trial of Pierce, Burgess and Tester, Testimony of Agar.
8 *Daily News*, 14 November 1856.
9 Trial of Pierce, Burgess and Tester, Testimony of Agar.
10 *Daily News*, 14 November 1856.
11 *Daily News*, 14 November 1856.
12 *Daily News*, 14 November 1856.
13 *Morning Chronicle*, 15 December 1856.
14 By Redhill he meant Reigate station: it had originally been called Redhill station.
15 Trial of Pierce, Burgess and Tester, Testimony of Russell.
16 Trial of Pierce, Burgess and Tester, Testimony of Perry.
17 Trial of Pierce, Burgess and Tester, Testimony of Perry.
18 Trial of Pierce, Burgess and Tester, Testimony of Perry.
19 Trial of Pierce, Burgess and Tester, Testimony of Russell.
20 Trial of Pierce, Burgess and Tester, Testimony of Russell.
21 Trial of Pierce, Burgess and Tester; *The Times*, 14 January 1857.
22 Gower was tried for the crime of embezzlement in October 1856 and sentenced to four years penal servitude. He had, though, no other connection with the train robbery itself.
23 Trial of Pierce, Burgess and Tester, Testimony of Agar.
24 Trial of Pierce, Burgess and Tester; *The Times*, 14 January 1857; *The Times* 14 November 1856.
25 *The Times*, 14 November 1856.

Chapter 10: Back Home

1 Trial of Pierce, Burgess and Tester, Testimony of Agar.
2 Trial of Pierce, Burgess and Tester, Testimony of Agar.
3 Trial of Pierce, Burgess and Tester, Testimony of Agar.

4 Trial of Pierce, Burgess and Tester, Testimony of Matthews.
5 Trial of Pierce, Burgess and Tester, Testimony of Matthews.
6 Trial of Pierce, Burgess and Tester, Testimony of Agar.
7 Trial of Pierce, Burgess and Tester, Testimony of Agar.
8 Trial of Pierce, Burgess and Tester, Testimony of Prommell.
9 Trial of Pierce, Burgess and Tester, Testimony of Agar.
10 *The Times*, 18 November 1856.
11 *The Times*, 18 November 1856.
12 *The Times*, 18 November 1856.
13 Trial of Pierce, Burgess and Tester, Testimony of Agar.
14 Trial of Pierce, Burgess and Tester, Testimony of Agar.
15 Trial of Pierce, Burgess and Tester, Testimony of Fanny Kay.
16 Trial of Pierce, Burgess and Tester, Testimony of Fanny Kay.
17 *The Times*, 18 November 1856.
18 *Hull Packet and East Riding Times*, 21 November 1856.
19 Trial of Pierce, Burgess and Tester, Testimony of Agar; *The Times*, 18 November 1856.
20 *The Times*, 18 November 1856.
21 *The Times*, 18 November 1856.
22 *The Times*, 18 November 1856.
23 *The Times*, 18 November 1856.
24 Trial of Pierce, Burgess and Tester, Testimony of Agar.
25 Trial of Pierce, Burgess and Tester, Testimony of Agar.
26 Trial of Pierce, Burgess and Tester, Testimony of Agar.
27 Trial of Pierce, Burgess and Tester, Testimony of Agar.
28 Trial of Pierce, Burgess and Tester, Testimony of Agar.

Chapter 11: Trust and Treachery

1 *The Times*, 9 December 1856.
2 *The Times*, 9 December 1856; he also received letters of recommendation from Superintendent P.D. Finnigan and a secretary, G.S. Herbert.
3 *The Times*, 9 December 1856.
4 *The Times*, 9 December 1856.
5 *The Times*, 9 December 1856.
6 *The Times*, 9 December 1856.
7 *The Times*, 9 December 1856.
8 Trial of Pierce, Burgess and Tester, Testimony of Fanny Kay.
9 Trial of Pierce, Burgess and Tester, Testimony of Fanny Kay.
10 Trial of Pierce, Burgess and Tester, Testimony of Fanny Kay.
11 Trial of Pierce, Burgess and Tester, Testimony of Fanny Kay.
12 Trial of Pierce, Burgess and Tester, Testimony of Agar.
13 Trial of Pierce, Burgess and Tester, Testimony of Agar.
14 *Liverpool Mercury*, 29 November 1856.

Chapter 12: Mansion House

1   *The Times*, 7 November 1856.
2   *The Times*, 7 November 1856.
3   *The Times*, 7 November 1856.
4   *The Times*, 7 November 1856.
5   *The Times*, 7 November 1856.
6   *The Times*, 7 November 1856.
7   *The Times*, 7 November 1856.
8   *The Times*, 7 November 1856.
9   *The Times*, 7 November 1856.
10 *The Times*, 7 November 1856.
11 *The Times*, 7 November 1856.
12 *The Times*, 7 November 1856.
13 *Era*, 30 November 1856.
14 *Era*, 30 November 1856.
15 *The Times*, 13 November 1856; *Glasgow Herald*, 17 November 1856.
16 *The Times*, 13 November 1856.
17 *The Times*, 13 November 1856.
18 *The Times*, 13 November 1856.
19 *The Times*, 13 November 1856.
20 *The Times*, 13 November 1856.
21 *The Times*, 13 November 1856.
22 *The Times*, 13 November 1856.

Chapter 13: One of a Class Too Numerous

1   *The Times*, 14 November 1856.
2   *The Times*, 14 November 1856; *Daily News*, 14 November 1856.
3   *Daily News*, 14 November 1856.
4   *The Times*, 14 November 1856.
5   *The Times*, 14 November 1856; *Daily News*, 14 November 1856.
6   *The Times*, 14 November 1856.
7   *The Times*, 18 November 1856.
8   *The Times*, 18 November 1856.
9   *The Times*, 18 November 1856.
10 *The Times*, 18 November 1856; *Hull Packet and East Riding Times*, 21 November 1856.
11 The following extract is from the report in *The Times*, 18 November 1856.
12 *The Times*, 18 November 1856.
13 *The Times*, 18 November 1856; *Caledonia Mercury*, 20 November 1856.
14 *The Times*, 18 November 1856.
15 *The Times*, 18 November 1856.

16   *The Times*, 18 November 1856.
17   *The Times*, 18 November 1856.
18   *The Times*, 18 November 1856.
19   *The Times*, 18 November 1856.
20   *The Times*, 18 November 1856.
21   *The Times*, 18 November 1856.
22   *The Times*, 18 November 1856.
23   *The Times*, 18 November 1856.

Chapter 14: The Promise of Return

1   *Belfast Newsletter*, 27 November 1856.
2   *Belfast Newsletter*, 27 November 1856.
3   *Daily News*, 25 November 1856.
4   *Daily News*, 25 November 1856.
5   *Daily News*, 25 November 1856.
6   *The Times*, 25 November 1856; *Daily News*, 25 November 1856.
7   *Daily News*, 25 November 1856.
8   *Belfast Newsletter*, 27 November 1856.
9   *Belfast Newsletter*, 27 November 1856.
10   *The Times*, 25 November 1856.
11   *The Times*, 25 November 1856.
12   *The Times*, 25 November 1856.
13   *Daily News*, 25 November 1856.
14   *The Times*, 25 November 1856; *Daily News*, 25 November 1856.
15   *Belfast Newsletter*, 27 November 1856; *Daily News*, 25 November 1856.
16   *Daily News*, 15 November 1856.
17   *Daily News*, 15 November 1856.
18   *Daily News*, 15 November 1856.
19   *Daily News*, 15 November 1856.
20   *The Times*, 25 November 1856; *Daily News*, 25 November 1856.
21   *Daily News*, 25 November 1856.
22   *The Times*, 3 December 1856.
23   *The Times*, 3 December 1856.
24   *The Times*, 3 December 1856.
25   *The Times*, 3 December 1856.
26   *The Times*, 3 December 1856.
27   *The Times*, 3 December 1856.

Chapter 15: A Voluntary Surrender

1   *The Times*, 9 December 1856.
2   *The Times*, 9 December 1856.
3   *The Times*, 9 December 1856.

4 *The Times*, 9 December 1856.
5 *The Times*, 9 December 1856.
6 *The Times*, 9 December 1856.
7 *The Times*, 9 December 1856.
8 *The Times*, 9 December 1856.
9 *The Times*, 11 December 1856.
10 *Daily News*, 11 December 1856.
11 *The Times*, 11 December 1856.
12 *The Times*, 11 December 1856.
13 *The Times*, 11 December 1856.
14 *The Times*, 15 December 1856.
15 *The Times*, 15 December 1856; *Daily News*, 15 December 1856.
16 *The Times*, 15 December 1856; *Daily News*, 15 December 1856.
17 *The Times*, 15 December 1856; *Daily News*, 15 December 1856.
18 *Daily News*, 15 December 1856.
19 *The Times*, 15 December 1856; *Daily News*, 15 December 1856.
20 *The Times*, 15 December 1856; *Daily News*, 15 December 1856.
21 *Daily News*, 15 December 1856.
22 *The Times*, 15 December 1856; *Daily News*, 15 December 1856.
23 *The Times*, 15 December 1856.
24 *The Times*, 15 December 1856; *Daily News*, 15 December 1856.
25 *The Times*, 15 December 1856; *Daily News*, 15 December 1856.
26 *The Times*, 15 December 1856; *Daily News*, 15 December 1856.

Chapter 16: A Case to Answer

1 *The Times*, 22 December 1856.
2 *Daily News*, 25 December 1856.
3 *The Times*, 22 December 1856.
4 *The Times*, 22 December 1856.
5 *The Times*, 25 December 1856.
6 *The Times*, 25 December 1856.
7 *The Times*, 25 December 1856.
8 *Daily News*, 25 December 1856.
9 *Hull Packet and East Riding Times*, 21 November 1856.

Chapter 17: Jim the Penman

1 *Examiner*, 10 January 1857.
2 *The Times*, 18 November 1856.
3 *Morning Chronicle*, 27 September 1858.
4 The Spellings 'Attwell' and 'Atwell' are both used in the documents.
5 Old Bailey Proceedings (www.oldbaileyonline.org), October 1856, trial
   of Hardwicke and Attwell, (t18561027-1004); Old Bailey Proceedings

(www.oldbaileyonline.org), March 1857, trial of Saward and Anderson, (t18570302-413).

6 *Leader – A Political and Literary Review.* 31/12/1857, vol. 8, no. 358.

7 Old Bailey Proceedings (www.oldbaileyonline.org), March 1857, trial of Saward and Anderson, (t18570302-413).

8 Old Bailey Proceedings (www.oldbaileyonline.org), March 1857, trial of Saward and Anderson, (t18570302-413).

9 Old Bailey Proceedings (www.oldbaileyonline.org), March 1857, trial of Saward and Anderson, (t18570302-413).

10 Old Bailey Proceedings (www.oldbaileyonline.org), March 1857, trial of Saward and Anderson, (t18570302-413).

11 Old Bailey Proceedings (www.oldbaileyonline.org), March 1857, trial of Saward and Anderson, (t18570302-413).

12 Old Bailey Proceedings (www.oldbaileyonline.org), October 1856, trial of Hardwicke and Attwell, (t18561027-1004); March 1857, trial of Saward and Anderson, (t18570302-413).

13 Old Bailey Proceedings (www.oldbaileyonline.org), March 1857, trial of Saward and Anderson, (t18570302-413).

14 Old Bailey Proceedings (www.oldbaileyonline.org), October 1856, trial of Hardwicke and Attwell, (t18561027-1004).

15 Old Bailey Proceedings (www.oldbaileyonline.org), March 1857, trial of Saward and Anderson, (t18570302-413).

16 Old Bailey Proceedings (www.oldbaileyonline.org), October 1856, trial of Hardwicke and Attwell, (t18561027-1004).

17 Old Bailey Proceedings (www.oldbaileyonline.org), October 1856, trial of Hardwicke and Attwell, (t18561027-1004).

18 Old Bailey Proceedings (www.oldbaileyonline.org), October 1856, trial of Hardwicke and Attwell, (t18561027-1004).

19 Old Bailey Proceedings (www.oldbaileyonline.org), October 1856, trial of Hardwicke and Attwell, (t18561027-1004).

20 Old Bailey Proceedings (www.oldbaileyonline.org), October 1856, trial of Hardwicke and Attwell, (t18561027-1004).

21 Old Bailey Proceedings (www.oldbaileyonline.org), October 1856, trial of Hardwicke and Attwell, (t18561027-1004).

22 Old Bailey Proceedings (www.oldbaileyonline.org), March 1857, trial of Saward and Anderson, (t18570302-413).

23 Old Bailey Proceedings (www.oldbaileyonline.org), October 1856, trial of Hardwicke and Attwell, (t18561027-1004).

24 Old Bailey Proceedings (www.oldbaileyonline.org), October 1856, trial of Hardwicke and Attwell, (t18561027-1004).

25 Old Bailey Proceedings (www.oldbaileyonline.org), October 1856, trial of Hardwicke and Attwell, (t18561027-1004).

26 Old Bailey Proceedings (www.oldbaileyonline.org), October 1856, trial of Hardwicke and Attwell, (t18561027-1004).

27 *Leader – A Political and Literary Review* – Town Edition, 14.02.1857, vol. 8, no. 360, p.151.
28 Old Bailey Proceedings (www.oldbaileyonline.org), March 1857, trial of Saward and Anderson, (t18570302-413).
29 Old Bailey Proceedings (www.oldbaileyonline.org), March 1857, trial of Saward and Anderson, (t18570302-413).
30 *Ipswich Journal*, 3 January 1857.
31 *Ipswich Journal*, 3 January 1857.
32 *Era*, 4 January 1857.
33 *Jackson's Oxford Journal*, 3 January 1857; *Ipswich Journal*, 3 January 1856.
34 *Ipswich Journal*, 3 January 1857.
35 *Examiner*, 10 January 1857.
36 *The Times*, 13 January 1857 quoting *The Law Times*.

Chapter 18: Cover-up

1 *The Times*, 27 November 1856; *Daily News* 26 November 1856; *Freeman's Journal and Daily Commercial Advertiser*, 28 November 1856.
2 *The Times*, 27 November 1856; *Daily News* 26 November 1856; *Freeman's Journal and Daily Commercial Advertiser*, 28 November 1856.
3 Trial of Pierce, Burgess and Tester, Testimony of Hazel.
4 Trial of Pierce, Burgess and Tester, Testimony of Hazel.
5 *The Times*, 11 December 1856.
6 *The Times*, 11 December 1856.
7 *Liverpool Mercury*, 29 November 1856 quoting *Morning Post*.
8 *The Times*, 15 December 1856.
9 *Daily News*, 26 November 1856.
10 *Daily News*, 26 November 1856.
11 *Daily News*, 26 November 1856.
12 Mr Bodkin at the Mansion House; *Morning Chronicle*, 14 November 1856; *Glasgow Herald*, 17 November 1856.
13 *Daily News*, 26 November 1856.
14 *Daily News*, 26 November 1856.
15 *Liverpool Mercury*, 29 November 1856, quoting from the *Morning Post*.
16 Trial of Pierce, Burgess and Tester, Testimony of Jones.
17 Trial of Pierce, Burgess and Tester, Testimony of Jones.
18 Trial of Pierce, Burgess and Tester, Testimony of Jones.
19 *Daily News*, 26 November 1856.

Chapter 19: The Trial

1 *The Times*, 14 January 1857.
2 *The Times*, 14 January 1857; Evans, p.507.

3 *The Times*, 14 January 1857.
4 *The Times*, 14 January 1857.
5 *The Times*, 14 January 1857.
6 *The Times*, 14 January 1857.
7 *The Times*, 14 January 1857.
8 *The Times*, 14 January 1857.
9 *The Times*, 14 January 1857.
10 *The Times*, 14 January 1857.
11 *The Times*, 14 January 1857.
12 *The Times*, 14 January 1857.
13 *The Times*, 14 January 1857.
14 *The Times*, 14 January 1857.
15 *The Times*, 14 January 1857.
16 *The Times*, 14 January 1857.
17 *The Times*, 14 January 1857.
18 *The Times*, 14 January 1857.
19 *Daily News*, 14 January 1857.
20 *Daily News*, 14 January 1857.
21 Trial of Pierce, Burgess and Tester, Testimony of Agar.
22 Trial of Pierce, Burgess and Tester, Testimony of Agar.
23 Trial of Pierce, Burgess and Tester, Testimony of Agar.
24 *The Times*, 14 January 1857.
25 *The Times*, 14 January 1857.
26 *The Times*; Agar says this later in reply to a question from Mr Sergeant Ballantine.
27 Trial of Pierce, Burgess and Tester, Testimony of Agar.
28 Trial of Pierce, Burgess and Tester, Testimony of Agar.
29 Trial of Pierce, Burgess and Tester, Testimony of Agar.
30 Trial of Pierce, Burgess and Tester, Testimony of Agar.
31 Trial of Pierce, Burgess and Tester, Testimony of Agar; *The Times*, 14 January 1857; *Daily News*, 14 January 1857.
32 Trial of Pierce, Burgess and Tester, Testimony of Agar.
33 Trial of Pierce, Burgess and Tester, Testimony of Agar.
34 Trial of Pierce, Burgess and Tester, Testimony of Agar.
35 Trial of Pierce, Burgess and Tester, Testimony of Agar.
36 Trial of Pierce, Burgess and Tester, Testimony of Agar.
37 Trial of Pierce, Burgess and Tester, Testimony of Agar.
38 *Daily News*, 14 January 1857.
39 *Daily News*, 14 January 1857.
40 *The Times*, 14 January 1857.
41 *The Times*, 14 January 1857.
42 Trial of Pierce, Burgess and Tester, *Daily News*, 14 January 1857.
43 *The Times*, 14 January 1857.
44 *The Times*, 14 January 1857.

45 *The Times*, 14 January 1857.
46 *The Times*, 14 January 1857.
47 *The Times*, 14 January 1857.
48 *The Times*, 14 January 1857.
49 *The Times*, 14 January 1857.
50 *The Times*, 14 January 1857.
51 *The Times*, 14 January 1857.
52 *The Times*, 14 January 1857.
53 *The Times*, 14 January 1857.
54 *The Times*, 14 January 1857.
55 *The Times*, 14 January 1857.

Chapter 20: Day Two

1 Trial of Pierce, Burgess and Tester, Testimony of Sharman.
2 *The Times*, 15 January 1857.
3 *The Times*, 15 January 1857.
4 *The Times*, 15 January 1857.
5 *Daily News*, 15 January 1857.
6 *The Times*, 15 January 1857.
7 *The Times*, 15 January 1857.
8 *The Times*, 15 January 1857.
9 *The Times*, 15 January 1857.
10 *The Times*, 15 January 1857.
11 *The Times*, 15 January 1857.
12 *The Times*, 15 January 1857.
13 *The Times*, 15 January 1857.
14 Trial of Pierce, Burgess and Tester, Testimony of Jones.
15 Trial of Pierce, Burgess and Tester, Testimony of Jones.
16 *The Times*, 15 January 1857.
17 *The Times*, 15 January 1857.
18 *The Times*, 15 January 1857.
19 *The Times*, 15 January 1857.
20 *The Times*, 15 January 1857.
21 *The Times*, 15 January 1857.
22 *Daily News*, 15 January 1857.
23 *The Times*, 15 January 1857.

Chapter 21: Intimately Acquainted

1 *The Times*, 15 January 1857.
2 *Daily News*, 15 January 1857.
3 *Daily News*, 15 January 1857.
4 Trial of Pierce, Burgess and Tester, Testimony of Fanny Kay.

5   Trial of Pierce, Burgess and Tester, Testimony of Fanny Kay.
6   Trial of Pierce, Burgess and Tester, Testimony of Fanny Kay.
7   Trial of Pierce, Burgess and Tester, Testimony of Fanny Kay.
8   Trial of Pierce, Burgess and Tester, Testimony of Fanny Kay.
9   In fact the child's birth and baptism were registered under the spelling 'Ager'.
10 *The Times*, 15 January 1857.
11 Trial of Pierce, Burgess and Tester, Testimony of Fanny Kay.
12 Trial of Pierce, Burgess and Tester, Testimony of Fanny Kay.
13 Trial of Pierce, Burgess and Tester, Testimony of Fanny Kay.
14 Trial of Pierce, Burgess and Tester, Testimony of Fanny Kay.
15 Trial of Pierce, Burgess and Tester, Testimony of Fanny Kay.
16 *The Times*, 16 January 1857.
17 Trial of Pierce, Burgess and Tester, Testimony of Fanny Kay.
18 *The Times*, 16 January 1857.
19 *The Times*, 16 January 1857.
20 Trial of Pierce, Burgess and Tester, Testimony of Carter.
21 Trial of Pierce, Burgess and Tester, Testimony of Carter.
22 Trial of Pierce, Burgess and Tester, Testimony of Carter.
23 Trial of Pierce, Burgess and Tester, Testimony of Knight.
24 *The Times*, 15 January 1857.
25 Trial of Pierce, Burgess and Tester, Testimony of Allday.
26 Trial of Pierce, Burgess and Tester, Testimony of Allday.
27 Trial of Pierce, Burgess and Tester, Testimony of May.
28 Trial of Pierce, Burgess and Tester, Testimony of May.
29 Trial of Pierce, Burgess and Tester, Testimony of May.
30 Trial of Pierce, Burgess and Tester, Testimony of Thompson.
31 Trial of Pierce, Burgess and Tester, Testimony of Lee.
32 *The Times*, 14 January 1857.
33 *The Times*, 15 January 1857.
34 Trial of Pierce, Burgess and Tester, Testimony of Knight.
35 Trial of Pierce, Burgess and Tester.
36 *The Times*, 15 January 1857.
37 Trial of Pierce, Burgess and Tester, Testimony of Raffan.
38 Trial of Pierce, Burgess and Tester, Testimony of Raffan.
39 Trial of Pierce, Burgess and Tester.
40 Trial of Pierce, Burgess and Tester, Testimony of Cousins.
41 Trial of Pierce, Burgess and Tester, Testimony of Rees.
42 *The Times*, 15 January 1857.
43 *The Times*, 15 January 1857; *Daily News*, 15 January 1857.
44 *The Times*, 15 January 1857.

Chapter 22: A Very Romantic Story

1 *The Times*, 16 January 1857.
2 *The Times*, 16 January 1857.
3 *The Times*, 16 January 1857.
4 *Morning Chronicle*, 16 January 1857.
5 *The Times*, 16 January 1857.
6 *The Times*, 16 January 1857.
7 *The Times*, 16 January 1857.
8 *The Times*, 16 January 1857.
9 *The Times*, 16 January 1857, referring to 'Rex V. Wilkes and Edwards'.
10 *The Times*, 16 January 1857.
11 Trial of Pierce, Burgess and Tester; *The Times*, 16 January 1857.
12 *The Times*, 16 January 1857.
13 Trial of Pierce, Burgess and Tester.
14 *The Times*, 16 January 1857.
15 *The Times*, 16 January 1857.
16 Trial of Pierce, Burgess and Tester.
17 *The Times*, 16 January 1857.
18 *The Times*, 16 January 1857.
19 *The Times*, 16 January 1857.
20 *The Times*, 16 January 1857.
21 *The Times*, 16 January 1857.
22 *The Times*, 16 January 1857.
23 *The Times*, 16 January 1857.
24 *The Times*, 16 January 1857.
25 *The Times*, 16 January 1857.
26 *The Times*, 16 January 1857.
27 *The Times*, 16 January 1857.
28 *The Times*, 16 January 1857.
29 Trial of Pierce, Burgess and Tester, *The Times*, 16 January 1857.
30 *The Times*, 16 January 1857.
31 *The Times*, 16 January 1857.
32 *The Times*, 16 January 1857.
33 Trial of Pierce, Burgess and Tester, *The Times*, 16 January 1857.
34 *The Times*, 16 January 1857.
35 *The Times*, 16 January 1857.
36 *The Times*, 16 January 1857.
37 *The Times*, 16 January 1857.
38 *The Times*, 16 January 1857.
39 *The Times*, 16 January 1857.
40 *The Times*, 16 January 1857.
41 *The Times*, 16 January 1857.
42 *The Times*, 16 January 1857.

43 *The Times*, 16 January 1857.
44 *The Times*, 16 January 1857.
45 *The Times*, 16 January 1857.
46 *The Times*, 16 January 1857.
47 *The Times*, 16 January 1857.
48 *The Times*, 16 January 1857.
49 *The Times*, 16 January 1857.
50 *Daily News*, 16 January 1857.
51 *Daily News*, 16 January 1857.
52 *The Times*, 16 January 1857.
53 *The Times*, 16 January 1857.
54 *The Times*, 16 January 1857.
55 *The Times*, 16 January 1857.
56 *The Times*, 16 January 1857.
57 *The Times*, 16 January 1857.
58 *The Times*, 16 January 1857.
59 Trial of Pierce, Burgess and Tester; *The Times*, 16 January 1857.
60 *The Times*, 16 January 1857.
61 *Daily News*, 16 January 1857.
62 *The Times*, 16 January 1857.
63 *The Times*, 16 January 1857.
64 *The Times*, 16 January 1857.
65 *The Times*, 16 January 1857.
66 *The Times*, 16 January 1857.
67 *The Times*, 16 January 1857.
68 *The Times*, 16 January 1857.
69 *The Times*, 16 January 1857.
70 *The Times*, 16 January 1857.
71 *The Times*, 16 January 1857.
72 *The Times*, 16 January 1857.
73 *The Times*, 16 January 1857.
74 *The Times*, 16 January 1857.
75 *The Times*, 16 January 1857.

Chapter 23: No Common Thief

1 *The Times*, 16 January 1857.
2 *The Times*, 16 January 1857.
3 *The Times*, 16 January 1857.
4 *The Times*, 16 January 1857.
5 *The Times*, 16 January 1857.
6 *The Times*, 16 January 1857.
7 *The Times*, 16 January 1857.
8 *The Times*, 16 January 1857.

9   *The Times*, 16 January 1857.
10 *The Times*, 16 January 1857.
11 *The Times*, 16 January 1857.
12 *The Times*, 16 January 1857.
13 *The Times*, 16 January 1857.
14 *The Times*, 16 January 1857.
15 *The Times*, 16 January 1857.
16 *The Times*, 16 January 1857.

Chapter 24: As Bad Can Be

1   Trial of Pierce, Burgess and Tester; *The Times*, 16 January 1857.
2   *The Times*, 16 January 1857.
3   *The Times*, 16 January 1857.
4   Trial of Pierce, Burgess and Tester; *The Times*, 16 January 1857.
5   Trial of Pierce, Burgess and Tester; Evans, p.499; *The Times*, 16 January 1857.
6   *The Autobiography of Samuel Smiles*.
7   *The Times*, 16 January 1857.
8   *The Times*, 16 January 1857.
9   *The Times*, 17 January 1857.
10 *Daily News*, 16 January 1857.
11 *The Times*, 16 January 1857.
12 *The Times*, 17 January 1857.
13 *The Times*, 16 January 1857.
14 *The Times*, 16 January 1857.
15 *The Times*, 16 January 1857.
16 *The Times*, 28 January 1857.
17 *The Times*, 28 January 1857; *Daily News*, 28 January 1857.
18 *The Times*, 28 January 1857.
19 *The Times*, 16 January 1857; *Daily News*, 28 January 1857.
20 *The Times*, 16 January 1857; *Daily News*, 28 January 1857.
21 *The Times*, 16 January 1857; *Daily News*, 28 January 1857.
22 *The Times*, 16 January 1857; *Daily News*, 28 January 1857.
23 *The Times*, 3 June 1858.
24 *The Times*, 5 February 1857.
25 *The Times*, 3 June 1858.
26 *Daily News*, 20 April 1857.
27 *Daily News*, 20 April 1857.
28 *Daily News*, 20 April 1857.
29 Records of Fremantle Prison, Western Australia, available at www.fremantleprison.com.au.
30 Records of Fremantle Prison, Western Australia, available at www.fremantleprison.com.au.

31 *The Times*, 16 January 1857.
32 *Morning Chronicle*, 26 January 1857.
33 *The Times*, 27 January 1857; *Daily News*, 27 January 1857.
34 *Morning Chronicle*, 16 February 1857.
35 *Morning Chronicle*, 26 February 1857; *Daily News*, 26 February 1857.
36 Old Bailey Proceedings (www.oldbaileyonline.org), (t18561027-1004).
37 *Morning Chronicle*, 27 September 1858.
38 *Morning Chronicle*, 27 September 1858.
39 *Daily News*, 13 December 1861.
40 *Daily News*, 13 December 1861.
41 *Leeds Mercury*, 27 December 1856.
42 Sekon, p.22.
43 Evans, p.485.